MW01687290

Phillip Knightley was born in Australia and has lived and worked in Britain, India, and the South Pacific. In 1981 he was named Journalist of the Year by the British Press Awards for his Vestey tax articles which were a factor in the government's decision to close the tax loophole. He writes and lectures on the press, propaganda, and espionage.

Also by Phillip Knightley:

PHILBY: The Life and Views of the KGB Masterspy

THE FIRST CASUALTY: The War Correspondent as Hero, Propagandist and Myth-maker from the Crimea to the Falklands

THE SECOND OLDEST PROFESSION: The Spy as Bureaucrat, Patriot, Fantasist and Whore

AN AFFAIR OF STATE: The Profumo Case and the Framing of Stephen Ward (co-author Caroline Kennedy)

The Rise and Fall of the House of Vestey

The true story of how Britain's richest family beat the taxman – and came to grief

Phillip Knightley

WARNER BOOKS

A *Warner* Book

First published in Great Britain in 1981 as
The Vestey Affair
by Macdonald & Co (Publishers) Ltd
This revised and updated edition published in 1993
by Warner Books
Reprinted 1994

A CIP catalogue record for this book
is available from the British Library.

ISBN 0 7515 0601 X

Typeset by
Hewer Text Composition Services, Edinburgh
Printed in England by Clays Ltd, St Ives plc

Warner Books
A Division of
Little, Brown and Company (UK) Limited
Brettenham House
Lancaster Place
London WC2E 7EN

For my father

Contents

List of Illustrations

Credit for the photographs is due as follows: Barratt's Photo Press (© S & G Press Agency Ltd) (1, 4); Desmond O'Neill (6); Barry Long (7); Hulton Deutsch Collection (8); Associated Press/Topham (9); Press Association/Topham (10, 11); *The Independent*/Steve Morgan (12).

Acknowledgements

I wish to thank Bruce Gates, who blazed the trail; Alan Jones for work in Liverpool; John McEwen (Scotland); Robert Lindley (Argentina); Coleen Ryan and Jane Cadzow (Australia); Jackie Williams (Paris); and Michael Kettle and Martyn Freeth (Britain). My colleagues on the *Sunday Times* gave me invaluable advice, assistance, and encouragement. I would like to mention, in particular, Harold Evans, Anthony Bambridge, John Barry, Don Berry, Tony Rennell, Antony Whitaker, Hugo Young, Stephen Fay, Edwin Taylor and Christopher Angeloglou.

I am grateful for permission to quote from various letters and articles. King George V's letter is published with permission, copyright reserved, and Lloyd George's reply by courtesy of the House of Lords' Record Office. Public Record Office material is published by permission of Her Majesty's Stationery Office.

Phillip Knightley
London, 1993

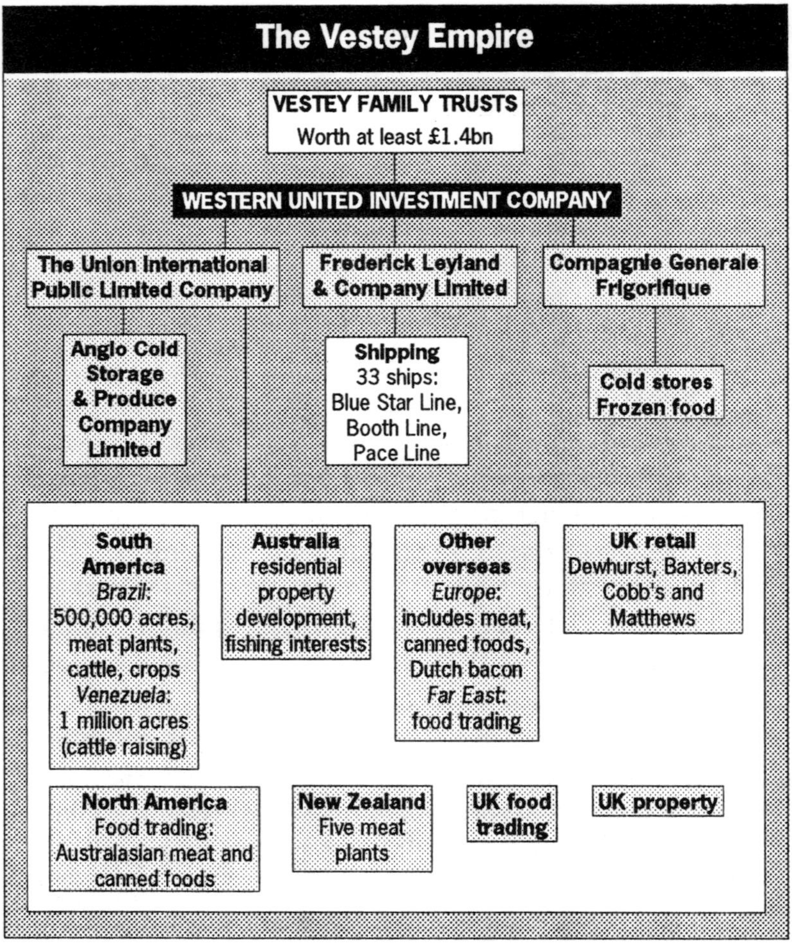
The Vestey Empire
VESTEY FAMILY TRUSTS
Worth at least £1.4bn
WESTERN UNITED INVESTMENT COMPANY
The Union International Public Limited Company
Frederick Leyland & Company Limited
Compagnie Generale Frigorifique
Anglo Cold Storage & Produce Company Limited
Shipping
33 ships: Blue Star Line, Booth Line, Pace Line
Cold stores
Frozen food
South America
Brazil: 500,000 acres, meat plants, cattle, crops
Venezuela: 1 million acres (cattle raising)
Australia
residential property development, fishing interests
Other overseas
Europe: includes meat, canned foods, Dutch bacon
Far East: food trading
UK retail
Dewhurst, Baxters, Cobb's and Matthews
North America
Food trading: Australasian meat and canned foods
New Zealand
Five meat plants
UK food trading
UK property

Introduction

In the autumn of 1991, Britain's business world was stunned to learn that Union International, one of the country's biggest and oldest private companies, was in desperate trouble. Union, the core company of the mega-rich Vestey family, owed about £423 million to some seventy banks and there was doubt that it could continue to meet its interest payments. 'Vestey Beg Bankers For More Time' said the headlines. 'Vestey Fortune Down £1bn – Losses Shake Beef Barons'. The first reaction was one of scepticism. Surely the world's richest butchers were not about to allow their company, part of the history of Britain's dominance of international commerce, to collapse? But as meeting after meeting with Union's bankers turned increasingly ugly – 'I never thought I'd hear language like that between banker and client,' said one observer – the truth emerged. Union had been ailing for a long while. The Vesteys had pumped £170 million into it and had decided that was enough. Now they were asking their bankers to share the burden; if they declined to co-operate, Union might well go to the wall.

Ten years earlier, the Vestey organisation was the biggest privately-owned multi-national in the world and the

Vesteys were Britain's richest family, worth an estimated £1,000 million. They owned family firms and properties in Argentina, Australia, Barbados, Belgium, Bermuda, Brazil, Canada, Cyprus, France, Germany, Holland, Hong Kong, India, Italy, Nigeria, New Zealand, Pakistan, Panama, Peru, Singapore, South Africa, Switzerland, Trinidad, the United Kingdom, the United States, Venezuela and Zimbabwe.

They were the world's biggest retailers of meat, the owners of Britain's biggest meat importing business, Weddel's, and the biggest meat retailing chain, Dewhurst; the largest manufacturers of clothing leather in the world, and the biggest supplier of own-brand margarine in Britain. They owned wool mills in Yorkshire, textile factories in Hong Kong and Australia, and cattle ranches in South America, Australia and New Zealand. The family had interests in property development, grocery wholesaling, supermarkets, guard dogs, insurance, shipping and travel. The family were pillars of the British establishment – friends of the Royal Family, peers of the realm, Old Etonians, High Sheriffs, Deputy Lieutenants of the county, Masters of the Hounds. Lord Vestey, fifty-two, Sam or even 'Spam' to his friends, liked to joke that he was the only butcher in the House of Lords, but at weekends he would often entertain the Waleses, the Westminsters, the Beauforts, the Astors, the Hoares and the Cobbolds. It would be hard to name a better-connected family.

So how was it that the Vesteys were now taking a begging bowl to the banks? What had gone wrong? One theory is that in 1980, the *Sunday Times* exposed what some say is a flaw in the Vestey family's business philosophy, one that had always been there but which had taken three generations to implode – dedication to massive tax avoidance. In a series of articles under the general heading 'The Gilded Tax Dodgers', the *Sunday Times* said that for more than sixty years the Vesteys had successfully but perfectly legally avoided paying millions of pounds of income tax.

It pointed out that other tax avoiders, like some pop stars and actors, had been forced into tax exile, but that the Vesteys had created a scheme which enabled them to live in Britain, enjoy British life, yet legally avoid paying large amounts of British tax. (The last, and unsuccessful, Inland Revenue demand on six members of the family was for income tax on £4.3 million and surtax on £7.3 million.) The articles quoted an Inland Revenue officer summing up his department's view on a sixty-year war of attrition with the family: 'Coming to grips with the Vesteys is like trying to squeeze a rice pudding.' The articles caused something of a sensation. Sam's cousin, Edmund, sixty-one, told the Press Association: 'Nobody pays more tax than they have to. We're all tax dodgers, aren't we?' The chairman of the Conservative Party, Lord Thorneycroft, defended the family: 'Good luck to anybody who can make a success of business,' he said. But the Chancellor of the Exchequer, Sir Geoffrey Howe, announced forty-eight hours later: 'We have immediately set in hand a review [of the tax loophole] and shall be introducing legislation to deal with it.' (He did in fact do so in the April 1981 Finance Bill.)

From the wealth of newspaper comment, letters, cartoons, television and radio phone-ins that followed, it was clear that the revelations about the Vesteys' tax arrangements had touched a tender nerve in the British conscience. Letters to newspapers in the following weeks showed that far from condemning what the Vesteys had done, most readers admired their initiative and ingenuity. A public debate raged over the ethics of tax avoidance in a highly-taxed society and spanned those who argued that everyone had not merely a right but a duty to avoid tax, to those who felt that the extent of tax avoidance represented an unfortunate decline in British moral standards.

But there is another point to be made – tax avoidance as a business strategy has its perils. As is made clear later in this book, the Vesteys devoted an enormous amount of time, energy and intellectual skill to their elaborate schemes for avoiding tax. If all this effort had instead been devoted to enterprise that could generate ample cash flow to expand and still pay tax, the Vesteys might not have got into financial difficulties. As it was, a detachment from the mainstream of British commercial life, an 'offshore' mentality – an essential part of tax avoidance – and a plan that required every decision to be examined in the light of its tax effectiveness, caused the Vesteys to take their eye off what they were good at, selling meat, with consequences we will examine.

There is a wider reason for the Vesteys' problems today, one that affects all Britain and can be seen as one of the causes of the nation's steady decline: Britain has never developed an urban or industrial aristocracy like many European countries. Here it has been traditional since late medieval times to put profits made in trade into land. This was originally done for greater security but later, on a growing scale, in a drive for respectability and gentility. (One exception was banking which was generally found to be compatible with membership of a landed aristocracy, as witness the Smiths, Barings, Barclays, Drummonds, Hambros and Rothschilds, who all continued successful banking businesses after their land acquisitions.) So powerful industrial and commercial families whose vigour could have further benefited the nation spent their wealth on land, joined the landed aristocracy and severed their links with the activity that had made them rich in the first place – the Peels and Arkwrights from cotton; the Marshalls from flax and linen; the Baileys and Crawshays from iron. Where the link was not totally cut, the commercial edge was generally lost.

This is what happened to the Vesteys. The Vestey brothers who made the family fortune, William (1859–1940) and Edmund (1866–1953) considered business not just a way of earning a living – it was life itself. They worked six days a week, kept modest houses and had no outside interests whatsoever. They did not live on income; they did not live on the interest from their investments; they lived on the interest on the interest. William believed business to be so important that when he was on honeymoon in Ceylon with his new wife, his former secretary, and there was a fire in the company packing plant in Rio, he sent her off to Rio on the next steamer.

William's great-grandson, Sam, the present Lord Vestey, has a grand country house, Stowell Park, Gloucestershire, set in 5,000 acres, and until recently devoted a large part of his life to polo and horse racing. At one time Lord Vestey had a helicopter to take him from his office to the polo field. An accountant estimated his living costs at £1 million a year. Edmund's grandson, Edmund Hoyle Vestey, is a hunting enthusiast, has a fine house in Saffron Walden, Essex, a farm in Hawick, Roxburghshire and a 100,000-acre estate at Assynt, Sutherland, Scotland. His father's estate at Great Thurlow in Suffolk contains a village and 11,000 acres of farmland.

In the folklore of the rich there is a truism – clogs to clogs in three generations: the first makes it, the second consolidates it, the third spends it. The Vesteys have avoided this because of the ingenuity of their predecessors in creating some 100 family trusts most of which are beyond the jurisdiction of the British taxman. They realised that what makes a family really rich is not how much it earns but how much it manages to keep. And a trust also acted as a safeguard against the profligacy of any one family member.

In 1992 there were about 250 beneficiaries to the Vestey trust funds, ranging from mainline family members to far-distant cousins. Some were so distant that they did not realise they were beneficiaries until, on their eighteenth birthday, they received a call to the Smithfield business headquarters of the family and were presented with a cheque for £250,000. Not everyone accepted; one bewildered girl said flatly, 'I can't handle it,' and turned it down.

When their tax affairs were revealed in 1980, the *Sunday Times* rated the Vesteys as the richest family in Britain. A conservative valuation then of their worldwide empire and the assets of their family trust, adjusted for inflation, produced a figure of £924 million, which was slightly below the estimate of informed financial experts. At that time the only rival in Britain to a fortune of that size was the Grosvenor family whose Westminster estate (London, Cheshire, Scotland, urban developments and Canada) was put at anything between £500 million and £2,000 million. But these figures needed to be qualified. The estate's London property consisted then of some 300 acres in Mayfair and Belgravia, most of it let out on ground leases. The £500 million to £2,000 million came from valuing the freehold of the properties when the leases expired. A more accurate view is that a long-deferred reversion has a minimal value – especially in the light of projected legislation that will, in effect, end leaseholds – and that it is better to value only the right to receive the current

rent and any likely increases. In this case the Grosvenors' fortune came out at about £1,000 million, neck and neck with the Vesteys. But as the Vesteys kept more of what they earned than the Grosvenors, the Vesteys emerged as top of the mega-rich league.

Twelve years later this appeared to have changed. *Business Age* did not even include the Vesteys in its 1992 list of Britain's ten richest men. Number one was either Paul Raymond, the Soho property landlord, striptease club owner and publisher of sex magazines, or David Sainsbury, head of the supermarket chain, depending on how you valued Soho property. Each man's fortune was estimated at between £1,500 million and £1,750 million. But the experts who compiled the table, and who excluded the Vesteys, underrated them. They made the mistake of equating the decline of the family's business with the family's personal fortune, which is squirrelled away in trusts, safe from the vicissitudes of Britain's economic ups and downs. We can only estimate how much is in these trusts, but based on projections from figures revealed in various Inland Revenue cases concerning the Vesteys, there was a conservative £1,317 million in 1993. Taking into account the Vesteys' assets in Britain and abroad, and the likelihood that there are other trusts as yet unrevealed, in my estimation the Vesteys are still Britain's richest family.

Top of the league or not, the Vesteys remain an amazing family. They fascinate us because they conform so neatly to the first rule of the game, defined so aptly by Peter Wilsher in his introduction to *The Rich and the Super Rich* – 'When you've got it, keep it' – and because, to apply F. Scott Fitzgerald's verdict on the rich, 'They are different from you and me.' Not just a little different, but very, very different, and this has had far-reaching effects. To take but two examples, it can be argued that in Argentina, the Vesteys' crippling effect on the Argentine labour movement and early economic development led almost directly to the formation of militant labour organisations that pushed Peron into power, the subsequent dictatorship of the generals, the terrorism, the Falklands War and the country's current economic disasters. In Australia, the novelist Xavier Herbert, in his epic novel *Poor Fellow My Country*, created a character called 'Lord Vaisey', the archetypal absentee British outback landlord, who exploits the land, pushes out the undercapitalised local pastoralist and destroys the aboriginal culture. The Vesteys – along with other British companies – were a factor in the rise of Australian nationalism – now reaching a climax with demands for a republic – and the belated recognition of aboriginal land rights.

In Britain, the Vesteys show that despite a well-publicised and apparently stringent tax system, the rich continue to pre-empt a very large share of society's resources – the swag is owned, by and large, by a group of less than a million people, most of whom have inherited it. Even in this elite group, the Vesteys have the edge. Their trustees do not just take out life insurance like ordinary people; they take out 'issue risk' on family members, insuring against any cousin having so many babies that she reduces the others' share when a trust fund is divided. And when Lord Vestey heard that the Queen had agreed to pay income tax, he smiled and said, 'Well, that makes me the last one.'

So who are the Vesteys? Where did they come from? How did they make their colossal fortune in the first place? Why has so little been known about them? How did they succeed in dodging tax? What are they really like? This book is an attempt to answer these questions.

1

Eggs from China

How the Vesteys became millionaires

The Vesteys have always been such a private, secretive family that many legends have grown up about where they came from and how they made their great fortune. One is that they started a grocer's shop in Liverpool about one hundred years ago, and that William, the first Lord Vestey, and his brother, Edmund, who became 'the millionaire meat kings', worked in the grocer's shop eighteen hours a day, seven days a week, to get a start in life. The truth is more prosaic. Their father, Samuel Vestey, was not a grocer but a well-to-do provisions broker who lived in a substantial house in Liverpool in the latter part of the nineteenth century. Originally from Yorkshire, he ran his business from 11 Trinity Road, Bootle, buying and selling provisions imported mainly from North America. Samuel was a man of considerable foresight and acumen, quick to appreciate how the mechanisation of agriculture and the mass production of crops in the United States would affect Britain's food supplies. He got in touch with American produce merchants, made one trip to the United States himself to organise his sources, and made a lot of money in a very short time. He married twice and in all had seven sons and five daughters. William was the eldest child, Edmund the fifth.

The two brothers entered their father's business at a time of great Victorian enterprise when the world was still Britain's oyster. Men with the knowledge, skill, and courage to go abroad and find new sources to supply Britain's increasing demand for food could make fortunes. So in 1876, old Samuel sent William to the United States to buy and ship home anything that the family could then sell in Liverpool.

William was seventeen. He had been brought up to respect the careful ways of his father and he was appalled when he visited the Chicago stockyards at the waste of perfectly edible meat. Americans, it seemed, wanted only the better cuts, and nutritious but unpopular parts of the beast were thrown aside as trimmings. So William bought the trimmings cheaply, arranged finance for a small canning plant from his father and began to ship corned beef to Liverpool. The business prospered and by 1882 William was back in Liverpool to marry a local girl, Sarah Ellis, and by 1889, when he was only thirty, he had made sufficient money to retire. He built a large house at Freshfield, near Southport, left his brother Edmund, who had been out to Chicago to learn the American end of the business, in charge, and settled down with his wife and three children to enjoy the life of a Victorian gentleman of leisure.

But not only did this bore him intensely, he felt that it was morally wrong. He was living largely on his income from the canning business and this was repugnant to him.

For if the Vesteys had one principal financial dictum it was never to live on current income: current income was for investment. As William told the Royal Commission on Taxation in 1919: 'I never spend any of my profits. I save every farthing. I live on what I earned twenty years ago.'

So William went back to work. First he went out to Argentina to see for himself how cattle were raised. As in Chicago, he was shocked by the waste. The Argentinians seemed interested in the cattle more for their hides than their meat and it was not unusual to see the carcase of a prime steer stripped of its hide and left to rot on the pampas. William noticed something else: partridges thrived in Argentina but the locals were big beef eaters and did not care for the birds. William reasoned that here was a chance for a quick profit. In Britain partridges were seasonal, luxury items, so if the birds could be sent to Liverpool there would be a good demand for them at a rewarding price.

William persuaded one of the local Argentinian freezing works, La Negra, to pack and freeze a trial shipment. It went well, so he returned to Liverpool to expand the marketing side of the business. At first the Vestey brothers stored the birds in a friend's cold store, but the business expanded so rapidly that the friend could no longer offer sufficient space, so the Vesteys took the step that was to set them on the road to unbelievable riches – they decided to build their own cold store. They bought some old cottages in Freemason's Row, gutted them, insulated the walls with cheap timber bought from Liverpool Docks, got a blacksmith to make heavy iron doors, installed the freezing machinery, and started in 1890 the cold store that was eventually to become Union Cold Storage, now Union

International, one of the largest cold storage operations in the world, and still the backbone of the Vestey empire.

There was more space in that first cold store than the Vesteys needed, so they approached the butchers and fishmongers in St John's market. In those days if a trader had not sold all his produce by Saturday evening, either he had to give it away or sell it cheaply for pig food because it would not keep fresh until Monday. For a modest charge the Vestey brothers offered to keep the meat and fish in their cold store so that the tradesmen would be able to eliminate waste. When all the cold store space was soon used for this business, the Vesteys built another one, in Banastre Street, to hold 4,000 tons of produce. Soon that, too, had all the business it could handle.

Which of the Vestey brothers then had the imagination to make the leap in their business affairs that took them from reasonably prosperous Liverpool merchants to a fortune of £20 million in ten years is hard to say. Probably it was Edmund. In later years when the Vesteys were famous, their business associates said that the two brothers complemented each other perfectly: Edmund had the flair, but could be reckless; William was the cautious, restraining hand. The thinking behind the leap was this: Britain had millions of industrial workers to feed. Yet in the early part of this century, production was seasonal, distribution poor, and, because cold storage was in its infancy, spoilage common. As a result, a lot of food items taken for granted today were either not regularly available or were beyond most people's means. In the present era of mass food production and nationwide distribution, it is difficult to imagine that before the First World War a housewife could not buy eggs regularly unless she happened to live near a poultry farm. Beef was a luxury, mutton expensive, poultry scarce. But the British consumer wanted meat rather than bread and potatoes. Demand steadily outstripped supply until it became obvious that the home market would never produce enough for Britain to feed itself.

Yet out there in the wide world were countries that were virtually gigantic farms worked by a peasant population that produced more than it could consume, anxious to sell to Britain to get currency to buy the highly-desirable manufactured goods that poured from British factories. The whole of northern China, for example, was one large poultry farm. So were many areas of Russia. Argentina was a huge cattle ranch. Australia and New Zealand produced sheep primarily for the wool, with mutton a secondary consideration. Bringing the two together – the industrial consumers of Britain and the primary producers in the other parts of the world – had not been possible before because the produce spoiled before it reached the market. But in the 1860s Charles Tellier invented an ammonia-compression refrigerating plant and in 1876 a shipment of meat from Argentina in a ship fittingly named *Le Frigorifique* reached France in edible – if not delectable – condition. Refrigerated ships and cold storage depots changed the face of the world food markets and the Vesteys were the first in Britain to realise it.

A cold store at a central point in the primary producing country would enable sufficient food to be gathered to justify chartering a refrigerated ship. In Liverpool the Vestey cold stores would be waiting to store the produce. Not only would all this make for efficient marketing, but it made marvellous business sense as well. Once the Vesteys had built a cold store in the producing country, they would have a virtual monopoly there because such an operation required considerable capital outlay and this would discourage competitors. With only the Vesteys to sell to, the producers would be forced to keep prices low. When the food arrived in Britain and the Vesteys' cold stores were well-stocked, they could assure tradesmen of a round-the-year supply. And since they could control the release of the foodstuffs to the market, they could stabilise the price and avoid the gluts and seasonal fluctuations that had made foodstuffs such a risky business.

The Vesteys started in Russia with cold stores in Riga, Petrograd and Moscow, then in China with depots at Hankow and Singargee (for a company they called the International Export Company) and at Shanghai (The Shanghai Ice and Cold Storage Company). They expanded their cold storage in Liverpool, eventually converting the old Theatre Royal, which had opened in 1772, causing the *Liverpool Daily Post* to comment, 'Somewhere amid all this beef and butter lurk the ghosts of Paganini, Charles Dickens, Grimaldi, and Henry Irving . . . ' Business boomed. In China, particularly, the profit margins were huge, for Chinese peasants did not want to be paid entirely in cash, which they mistrusted, but with rice or with goods, mainly paraffin and denim cloth which the Vesteys could buy cheaply in Britain.

The Vesteys's first man in China was E. Caesar Gill, but little is known about him. Then came Joe Mather, known to all as 'Joe Egg'. Mather went out from Wallasey to found a barter trade that could have come from the Middle Ages. First he had to find and do a deal with the local war lord, the only man with the power and organisation to guarantee that the peasants would keep their side of the contract. The Vesteys wanted hen and duck eggs, chickens, rabbits and sheep. On his occasional return visits to Liverpool, Mather used to show other Vestey employees photographs of Chinese duck farms, thousands of ducks that had been driven from the surrounding countryside swimming in huge pools or lagoons. The farmers brought their surplus to Mather and his Chinese employees packed the eggs in rice husks in wooden boxes, 720 or 1,440 to a box (multiples of a dozen, the basic retail package) and shipped them in the chilled space in a refrigerated ship.

But shipping Chinese eggs in the shell had one remaining disadvantage: it was still a seasonal trade because the fierce Chinese winters slashed production. This made the baking industry a seasonal one also. Cakes like sponges and Swiss rolls were marketed only intermittently in those days. The only type of cake sold all year round was fruit cake or Dundee cake because it could be baked when eggs were available and sealed in tins. It is no accident that a traditional English afternoon tea has a 'heavy' cake rather than a Swiss roll. So the Vesteys began breaking the eggs in China, mixing them with a giant egg whisk, freezing the beaten egg in large tins and shipping this mix to Liverpool for sale to the catering trade. This simple step revolutionised the British baking business – for the first time it could bake 'light' cakes all the year round – and was one of the factors in the growth of catering giants like Joe Lyons.

But the Vesteys' China trade was not smooth-running all the time. For example, on one occasion they bought 50,000 sheep in the Kweihwa district only to find that when they tried to drive them overland to their depot at Tientsin, civil war had broken out and the roads were cut. So they got permission from the local official in charge of foreign affairs, a Mr Pao, to hold the sheep where they were, Pao promising to give them his full protection. But, as the Vesteys later reported to the British Foreign Office: 'Mr Pao then left the district, and after long-drawn-out negotiations, our sheep were confiscated by the Governor of Suiyan after we had refused to pay him a "squeeze" of $60,000.' The Vesteys tried to get their money back from the central Chinese government, but they were unsuccessful.

The egg trade with Russia and China continued until the Second World War and at its peak Britain was importing 40,000 tons of frozen eggs a year. For the Vestey brothers it was the door to bigger and better business. But they never forgot the part that frozen eggs had played. When William became a peer he acknowledged the family's debt by incorporating in his coat of arms an unusual heraldic feature: three eggs supported by an iceberg.

The Vesteys' second rule for success in business was: never let other people do anything for you which you can do for yourself. So when one shipment of eggs from China, sent on a regular steamer which had been delayed at an intermediate port, arrived in Liverpool so bad they had to be dumped, the Vesteys began to look around for ships of their own. In 1909 they bought two second-hand refrigerated cargo steamers which had been on the New Zealand run, the *Pakeha* and the *Rangatira*. They renamed them *Broderick* and *Brodmore* and on July 28, 1911 registered the Blue Star Line Ltd with offices in London and Liverpool and a capital of £100,000. Expansion was now very rapid. In the next three years the Vesteys bought five more ships, a butchery business with a chain of retail shops in Britain and small freezing works in Australia and New Zealand. They were now well on the way to the totally-integrated business operation that is today a distinguishing feature of the Vestey empire. By owning every link in the chain between producer and consumer the Vesteys were able to keep the profit each link produced to themselves. So by 1914 William and Edmund, in the cold storage business for not quite twenty-five years, had made £10 million each – the equivalent in today's values of £240 million.

Business for them became not just a way of earning a living; it was life itself. They had no outside interests whatsoever. Neither brother drank nor smoked. They resolutely turned down opportunities to enter the wine and spirit business, they kept close watch to make certain that no employee drank during business hours, and they inspected the fingers of their staff regularly for signs of tobacco stains. They dressed inconspicuously in dark business suits with waistcoats, watch and chain, and Homburg hats. They ate frugally and when business required them to eat out they preferred a cheap meal at an ABC café. They had no extravagances. William was fond of telling new recruits to the Vestey empire that before he got rich, when he was earning only £20,000 a year, he put aside £19,500 for investment and he, his wife, and their four children lived on the remaining £500.

The Vesteys worked six days a week. On Sunday they would go to church, eat Sunday lunch with their families and then meet to study all the financial newspapers. If they found a company that appeared to be making a good profit, they would buy it. A former employee remembers, 'They were always on the look out for an old-established family business. They got all the old-time butchers this way – Eastmans, Dan Higgins, Fletchers. They'd read the papers and they'd seen Higgins making a lot of money and they'd say, "Let's buy him over." And if the butcher was an elderly man and getting tired running the business they'd get it for a song. They never kept any of their money. As soon as they had any they'd use it to buy someone over. If they found a firm making a good profit and they couldn't buy him over then they'd go into the same line of business in competition with him. They'd have a go at anything.'

As their business expanded it was impossible for the Vesteys to do everything themselves, so they developed a system of encouraging their brighter, ambitious employees to do it for them. They would send word to their district managers that they were looking for someone to go to Argentina or Brazil, either to start a new business or to run an established one. The same former employee remembers, 'If I had a reasonably intelligent young man I'd send him along for an interview. If they liked the look of him they'd send him out on a contract, offer him £100 a year more than he was getting. In those days most of them would jump at it, especially a single man with a taste for a bit of adventure. They got into bananas in Brazil this way. Sent a young man out there. You explore the possibilities and let us know. They got the seed from the Canaries and crossed it with Jamaican. They eventually built up a big business with an office in Liverpool under the name of Howard Chapman and Co. That was the sort of thing they'd do. Once they got it into their minds that there was money in something there was no stopping them. Other businessmen hated them. They would never use their own name but always one of their associated companies. But the word got around. I would call on someone and he'd say, "You're Vesteys, aren't you? We're not doing business with them. They're in everybody's business and they want everybody's business."'

The Vesteys' attitude to their own employees was a confusing mixture of paternalism and financial meanness. If an employee was loyal he was repaid with concern – not cash. One of the Liverpool typists, now in her eighties, recalls, 'Every Monday I had to work out the percentages of profits for all the meat shops and get them in the 3 p.m. post to William in London. We had one meat shop manager who couldn't read or write. Yet how he could make a profit! That's where the Vesteys weren't snobs. They wanted someone to do the job. If he could do it, then that was fine. They didn't care whether a man could read or write. They used to give us an annual dinner at the Adelphi Hotel, Liverpool. Seven or eight courses with red and white wine. It was organised so that afterwards people could dance or play cards. The Vesteys never danced themselves. They went around shaking hands and chatting. There were always a few speeches and the Vesteys thanked everyone for pulling their weight for the firm.'

But there was no proper pension scheme until after the Second World War. Before then it was up to the Vesteys to decide whether an employee would receive anything when he became too old to work. A former manager explains how the system worked: 'I remember a manager in the twenties, who was getting about £700 a year, going to see the Vesteys about his retirement. He was offered perhaps a pound or two a week. They'd want to know all about your family history. Was your wife dead or alive? Any children? Daughter? Is she married? No? Then she can keep you. No, I'm not depending on my daughter and I can't manage on a pound a week. You'd have to make your case and try to get a bit more. Perhaps if the offer was a pound then you might get thirty shillings. It was the same with wages. There was a twice yearly review. The managers would have to send in a list. I'd put down a figure for a weekly rise, five shillings, seven and sixpence and so on. The Vesteys didn't care how useful someone was to me, they only looked at the figures. Then they'd cut them back and I'd end up losing a good man. Once I gave a foreman ten bob a week without telling London. I thought no one would notice. But Edmund was on the telephone within days. Who authorised this? I got my knuckles rapped.'

2

The Move to Argentina

The first scheme to avoid tax

The outbreak of war in 1914 brought a further boost to the Vestey fortunes. William had been made a baronet in 1913 for his role in making cheap food more widely available in Britain. Now, with hundreds of thousands of troops pouring into Kitchener's army, there was an enormous demand for provisions suitable for troops: bully beef, tongue, eggs, tinned fruit, frozen meat – the very basis of the Vestey empire. The British government had announced immediately after the outbreak of war that it would make all of the country's meat purchases and in January, 1915, Britain also started buying for France. In Argentina alone, the total slaughter of cattle for export doubled between 1914 and 1918 and by the last year of the war Allied troops were consuming up to one million pounds of meat a day.

All this had to be stored somewhere, so the Vesteys put their cold storage facilities at Boulogne, Le Havre and Dunkirk at the disposal of the Allies and with financial help from the British government they built more cold stores in Liverpool and Glasgow and poured food into them. The Alexandra Dock project in Liverpool could handle 20,000 tons of produce and was at the time the largest cold store in Europe. The Vesteys did not *make* their fortune in 1914–1918, but the war helped them to consolidate and grow. The statistics tell the story. They began the war with cold stores in Britain, Russia and China, and with seven ships, four of which were refrigerated. By 1919 they had ranches, plants, and cold stores in Australia, New Zealand, South Africa, Madagascar, France, Spain and Portugal, and the Blue Star Line had acquired five more ships. The single most important expansion was in Argentina, where in 1915 the Vesteys began converting a large works called Las Palmas which had been built in the late 19th century at Zarate on the river Parana northwest of Buenos Aires. This was the foothold in Argentina that the Vesteys needed in order to compete with the American meat giants like Swift and Armour.

But the same year that the Vesteys decided that they were ready to compete with the Americans something happened in Britain that changed the family's course: the British government introduced new laws about company taxation and increased income tax and death duties. Until then, if a British-based company made profits abroad, it was not taxed on those profits unless it brought them back to Britain. The 1914 Finance Act, designed to raise the huge amounts of money needed to wage war against Germany, changed that: even if the company kept those profits abroad it now had to pay British tax on them. The

Vesteys were outraged. Their principal competitor was the American Beef Trust (founded in the 1880s by the 'robber baron' Philip D. Armour, described as a 'puritanical and grasping dealer in pigs'; he is quoted as outlining his business philosophy: 'I like to turn bristles, blood and the inside and outside of pigs into revenue.'). The Trust, as a foreign company, paid no company tax in Britain, and, unless the Trust remitted its foreign profits to the USA, it paid no tax there either. The Vesteys thought it was unfair that their foreign rival could trade in Britain and keep more of its profits than a native English company could. Income tax was increased from 1*s* 2*d* in the pound to what they saw as a scandalous 3*s* – and death duties were, the Vesteys believed, even worse. For the British government to tax their company profits, then to tax that same money again as income, and finally to tax it yet again as death duties – 'just deferred income tax', said William – was diabolical. William did a calculation. It ignored the allowance for the standard rate of company taxation, then nine per cent, and included death duties as if they were payable immediately. It added up to a grim picture for a family which had come to regard every hard-earned penny as its own. Out of every £100 profit, William calculated that the family would have to pay 40 per cent excess profits tax. This left £60, from which income tax and super tax would take away another £31.10*s*. Of the remaining £28.10*s*, death duties at 40 per cent would leave the Vesteys only £17.2*s* 'to cover the use of our capital, to cover the risk, and as payment for our time, energy, and enterprise.'

(William's inclusion of death duties in this calculation had a strong emotional reason. His father, Samuel, had died in 1902 and by the judicious transfer of his assets to his children before his death had nothing to leave, no will to make, and no death duties to pay.)

At first the Vesteys thought that William's figures would constitute an irrefutable argument and, coupled with their help for the war effort, would make the government see reason. They were sufficiently influential – William was known in Whitehall as well as in the meat trade – to obtain interviews with high-ranking Treasury officials and the president of the Board of Trade, Sir John Bradbury, but they came away disappointed. The Treasury was sympathetic, but well aware that any exemption such as the Vesteys sought could undermine the whole basis of taxation. The Vesteys would have to smile and pay. After all, as one Treasury official told them, taxation would not *stop* the Vesteys from earning profits; so surely their real grievance was that the family's business rivals would *keep* more profit than they would.

It was probably this remark which crystallised the Vesteys' thinking on their future. They were far-sighted enough to realise that many of the tax increases – supposedly only wartime measures – were here to stay. In the future what would distinguish the real rich of Britain would be not how much they made, but how much they were able to keep. It was November, 1915, the second year of the war. The Vesteys, gripped by their revelation about taxation and determined not to let the government take all but £17.2*s* from every £100 they made, packed up and left Britain.

First they went to Chicago, a city they knew well, where they consulted a lawyer who had been recommended to them by American friends as an expert on tax matters. How, William asked him, could the Vesteys dodge this new British taxation? The Chicago lawyer was not only sympathetic, he was experienced. As William recalled later, he told the Vestey brothers, 'What's the matter with your people? You are the third Englishman I've had in here this week on the same business.' The following month, with help from the American lawyer and advice from William's private secretary, Edward Brown, who was to prove a genius on tax affairs, the Vesteys set up a scheme that achieved all that they wanted. It enabled them to run their worldwide business from Argentina, where they remained until the end of the war, keep their main British company, Union Cold Storage, collect the profits from their business, and pay tax on only a fraction of those profits.

The scheme worked like this. First the Vesteys set up an American company, National Cold Storage of New York, in which they held the controlling interest. Their British company, Union, then signed an agreement to give National the use of all the Vestey overseas empire. In return National agreed to pay sufficient money for Union to meet its fixed charges and to maintain its dividends, a total at that time of about £224,000 a year. As far as Britain was concerned, those profits which had previously been the Vesteys' and subject to British tax, now became the profits of a foreign company, National, and since the money did not come to Britain, no British tax was due on them. The profits did not go to the United States, either, so no American tax was due on them there. They went instead to the owners of National, none other than the Vestey brothers. The Vesteys were living in Argentina where, conveniently, there was no income tax at all. So the Vesteys ended up paying nothing.

Of course, Union still had to pay company taxes in Britain, and there was no way that the Vesteys could avoid that obligation. But they did their best to minimise their tax bill. They tried to argue that since Union had not *leased* the Vestey overseas business to National, but had merely *agreed* to allow National to *use* them, then, in law, Union remained responsible for all the overseas buildings and plant and had an obligation to insure them and, eventually, to replace them. So they claimed as deductible running expenses for Union the insurance and depreciation charges for these overseas assets. These deductions reduced Union's profits – and therefore its taxes – considerably. The Inland Revenue did not agree with the Vesteys' argument and took them to court.

There the Vesteys' explanation was ingenious. They said that in 1915 they had become worried about the future of the Russian trade which had contributed nearly half Union's profits. They doubted whether this could continue. They were also having difficulty with cables and transport between Britain, the United States, China and other countries, and as America was not engaged in the war at that time they thought that an American company would be in a better position to cope with these difficulties than Union. This explanation was not entirely accepted by Lord Justice Atkin when the case reached the Court of Appeal. 'The agreement . . . between Union and the National Company is certainly of a very remarkable character such as I personally have never had occasion to see before. There can be very little doubt but there must have been considerations leading to the formation of that agreement . . . other than the considerations accepted by the [Taxation] Commissioners and accepted by us.' The Court found against the Vesteys; one of the few legal battles they have ever lost.

In Argentina the Vestey brothers set up offices in

an impressive nine-storey building at Reconquista 46, with the Strangers' Club, a meeting place for British expatriates, as their neighbours. They later moved to even more important offices at Avenida Roque Saenz Pena (Diagonal Norte), third floor. All the profits they collected from National they ploughed into the Zarate works, and when that was finished, into other packing plants. The Vestey company was known locally as *el Inglés* and one Argentinian, writing in Spanish about the Vestey operations, tried to capture the energy the family put into this period of wartime expansion. '*El Inglés* bought and sold packing houses as though they were so many lots of steers. As can be imagined, the juggling acts that *el Inglés* performed with packing houses were enough to give the best aviator a dizzy spell. So it is not surprising that the company tax inspector had a difficult job to unravel it all when *el Inglés*, in the end, was left with just one packing house. In effect, the Vestey company was a native corporation with insignificant capital because all it did was to rent a packing house. The owner was the home office in England.'

This single packing house was the Anglo-Buenos Aires, at South Dock, just outside the city limits on the River Plate estuary. It was not finished until late 1926 but it was the largest and most modern in the world. The wartime profits that enabled the Vesteys to build this packing house and to expand their empire were directly boosted by the British government. Many Argentinians were angered by the staggering amounts of money which packing houses were making in Argentina, hated seeing the prosperity of the national industry, cattle, enriching foreigners and felt humiliated by the conditions under which Argentine nationals had to work in this industry.

They despised highly-placed Anglophiles, such as the law firm of Dr Horacio Beccar Varela, who acted for the Vesteys as well as for the Americans Swift and Armour, and called them 'sepoys'. Occasionally these feelings erupted into violence. There would be a series of strikes on the railroads, in ports and in the British-owned meat-packing plants. The response was always the same. The Vesteys would complain to the Foreign Office in London which in turn would ask the British Ambassador to request the Argentine Ministry for Foreign Affairs to provide adequate police protection for the companies. Upholding the time-honoured right of free men to work when and where they wanted, the ambassador would deplore violence, point out that the strike was caused by 'German-inspired agitators', and emphasise the importance of meat supplies for the Allied war effort. The Argentine government would readily comply, the strikes would be broken, and the workers would have to return to their jobs with little or no change in pay or conditions.

The Foreign Office was less vigorous, however, when in 1917 the United States became worried over the ultimate destination of a shipment of 2,000 tons of refined lard belonging to the Vesteys. The United States Food Administration, in charge of the American end of the economic blockade against Germany, intercepted a telegram from the Chicago branch of the Vesteys offering the lard, from the Nanking province of China, for sale to the Norwegian government. Norway was neutral during the war and the Americans were worried that the lard might end up in Germany. They told the Foreign Office that they hoped 'such transactions will not be permitted by British firms pending negotiations with Norway'. The Contraband Section at the Foreign Office said that it did not see how it could prevent British firms negotiating deals like this, 'nor the object in doing so as neutrals are not dependent on us in these matters'. The Contraband Section memorandum on the matter went on: 'We can, of course, discourage negotiations in particular cases such as this, which are brought to our notice and we can put difficulties in the way of the actual shipments. We will reply as above to Washington and ask Messrs Vestey by telephone to cause their Chicago branch to drop these negotiations.'

But the Vesteys came from a tough mould. As recorded in the Foreign Office archives, the affair came to a quick end. 'I have communicated with Messrs Vestey,' wrote the Foreign Office official in charge of the case. 'They say that beyond the fact that the American firm, which is a separate entity, holds shares in the London firm, there is no connection between them, and they are not in a position to control the actions of the American firm.' The Vestey brothers could, of course, have stopped the shipment if they had wanted to – they had total control of all their overseas businesses – but they were able to do what they thought best for the Vesteys by hiding behind the secret, complicated structure of their empire. Nothing was done to stop 'the Chicago branch', and the lard went to Norway. What happened to it then is not known.

It is worth noting at this stage of the Vestey story that the Vesteys were not the only family business to make money during the war. Families in steel, shipping, munitions, transport – all the industries without which a national war machine cannot function – inevitably made large profits. Some felt a sense of guilt. The future Prime Minister, Stanley Baldwin, who was in 1919 a junior minister at the

Treasury, calculated that his family steel mills at Wilden and in South Wales had made something like £600,000 profit from the war. Inspired by the government's vision of a reconstructed Britain, 'a land fit for heroes', Baldwin wrote an anonymous letter to *The Times* proposing that he should donate one-fifth of these profits – £120,000 – to the nation, by buying government stock and giving it to the Treasury, if others would do likewise. His offer met with a resounding silence and it is unlikely Baldwin went ahead.

William later argued in Parliament that although the Vesteys had been in Argentina for most of the war, they had nevertheless done their bit for the war effort by putting their cold storage facilities at the Allies' disposal. But the exact circumstances surrounding this deal remained vague until 1922 when, as we shall see, the government revealed that the Vesteys' war-time role was not all they had claimed.

3

The Paris Trust

William and Edmund create a masterpiece

William and Edmund returned to Britain in February, 1919. It had been a long exile, but even in the emotional flush of a home-coming they took certain precautions to ensure that for tax purposes they were only visitors. 'I am technically abroad at present,' William told someone who asked him whether he had come back to Britain to live. The first thing that the Vesteys did was to write a long letter to the Prime Minister, Lloyd George. William signed it, but it reflects the family thinking. Dated February 22, 1919, it was an impassioned plea to be exempted from the tax laws. The Vesteys dressed this plea with appeals to patriotism, fair competition, and the relief of unemployment, but underneath it was a straight personal request to the leader of the country to order the Inland Revenue not to tax the Vesteys like other citizens.

The object of this letter is to set before you the

> impossible position in which our purely English firm of Vestey Brothers is placed owing to the freedom from taxation given to the American Beef Trust on practically the whole of their business in England, while we should have to pay away almost the whole of any income we might derive from the business, and as the Revenue officials have already been discussing for fifteen years the question of taxation of the American Beef Trust, to ask if equality of treatment cannot be given to us now while we are alive.

The letter went on to set out the extent of the Vestey empire and to explain how taxation in 1915 had made it impossible for the Vesteys to continue working in Britain. William then returned to the American Beef Trust.

> They are fierce competitors with more than £100 million of capital, enterprising and skilled in the business and with the whole force of the American Government and of every employee of that Government everywhere working like beavers for them. Under these circumstances for any firm to try to compete with them on anything but absolutely equal terms is useless; the slightest handicap means failure. All our lives we have been working in the same markets as the Trust quite successfully and so long as we live abroad or if you can permit us to return to England, we expect to be able to continue to do so.

The letter then set out William's calculations showing that the family would have to pay £92.8*s* in tax on every £100 the brothers earned. It contrasted this with the fact that the Beef Trust paid no tax on 90 per cent of their business with Britain and only a trifle on the remaining ten per cent.

> We are told that the Government would like to get England out of the clutches of the American Beef Trust but in fact the Trust themselves could never have conceived so perfect and simple a device for consolidating and extending their practical monopoly of the frozen meat trade as that the British Government should exempt them from taxation and impose a tax of £92.8*s* per cent on the profits of any British firms which have the temerity to oppose them. It appears impossible but that is the present position.

William said he was willing to bring his company back to Britain if Lloyd George would give an assurance that the Vesteys would be taxed at the same rate as the American Beef Trust.

> The Government will not lose any revenue by allowing us to return; they are not receiving any now and never can under the above conditions, whereas if we return they will receive many thousands of pounds annually from business we shall do in England, in addition to the death duties we must pay and which sums they will lose if we die domiciled abroad. Further, should we be permitted to return, we shall find work for 3,000 to 5,000 Englishmen, instead of that number of foreigners abroad. We ask for no preference, advantage, or assistance in any way, merely an equal chance in our own country, and it does seem to me that that an Englishman who only wants to work, should have to petition for equality

of treatment with a foreigner, is a most pitiable thing.

Lloyd George was not moved. He got William off his back – he was pressing for an interview – by suggesting that the Vesteys should give evidence before the Royal Commission on Income Tax. William duly appeared on July 31, 1919. It was a mistake. He met with some polite but hostile questioning from Commission members and, provoked, he lost his composure and gave away more than he had intended. It is important to look at his evidence in some detail because contained in his answers are clues not only to his personal attitude to taxation but to the whole theory behind the structure of the present-day Vestey empire.

William began by saying that if the government continued its taxation policies then there would soon cease to be any revenue from English freezing works abroad because they would be taxed out of existence, no new ones would start, and the American Beef Trust, aided by the British government, would have secured a monopoly of the supply of foreign beef to England. He said that what he really wanted was a return to the pre-1915 position: that income arising from the Vesteys' operations abroad and not brought into Britain should be free of tax. He admitted that such a concession would affect many other British firms and that the loss of this tax would make a serious gap in the government's revenue. But he objected to the tax on principle: 'If I kill a beast in the Argentine and sell the product of that beast in Spain, this country can get no tax on that business. You may do what you like, but you cannot have it.' The Commissioners pressed him on this view.

You would not object to be assessed on your foreign

profits which you sent over to this country? – The net result would be that none whatsoever would be sent over.

I suppose that you would not object to this: assessment on your business excluding the trading between foreign companies? – In a business of this nature you cannot say how much is made in one country and how much is made in another. You kill an animal and the product of that animal is sold in fifty different countries. You cannot say how much is made in England and how much abroad.

Where are you domiciled at present. In this country? – No, Buenos Aires. I am technically abroad at present, but I came over here specially to appear before this Commission. The present position of affairs suits me admirably. I am abroad; I pay nothing. I am talking against my own interest, but I was born in the good old town of Liverpool and I want to die in this country, and I want to come and work here; that is why I am here. Really I am doing myself harm by making all these propositions. If I have got to live abroad I am speaking against myself.

One of the Commissioners asked William about income tax. Did he realise that it was tax on individual income? William said that he did, but he considered that he would have already paid it in his firm's profit tax. The exchange then grew heated.

Commissioner: No, you would still have to pay it because you are a resident here. Are you not to pay anything for the advantage of living here? – *No answer*.

Commissioner: With respect, I should like to have

an answer. It is one that has agitated me a good deal since the witness has been in the chair.

Chairman: Sir William is going to give an answer. I think he was indicating it by gesture. (*To witness*) You are prepared, of course, to pay income tax as a resident upon your income, are you not? – Yes, I think I must say so.

At the end of William's evidence, one Commissioner tried to sum up.

Does not your whole objection on this amount to an objection to the graduated income tax? Is not your real complaint that each source of income should be treated by itself, and that nothing extra should be levied upon the taxpayer because his total incomes lumped together are larger than his neighbour's income? – No, I never thought about that. My sole point is that I should not be called upon to pay more than the American Beef Trust pay.

Your real grievance is that whether it hurts your pocket or not, it hurts your feelings very badly to be trading alongside a competitor who is not taxed as heavily as you are? – I have no doubt it does; it makes me very cross.

It must have soon been obvious to the Vesteys that the British government had no intention of exempting them from any form of taxation, so they set about achieving what they wanted in their own way. The clues to how they did it lie in some of William's answers to the Royal Commission and in the nature of the meat business. Although an outsider in this business would imagine that the largest slice of the profits would go to the cattle rancher, the man who has bred and raised the beast, this is not so. Cattle raising requires wide, open spaces and, by definition, these are a long way from the main markets for meat: the heavily-populated industrial areas of the northern hemisphere. The man who turns a live beast into food products ready for sale in these markets, the meat packer, is the man in control of the operation and, as a result, the major profit-maker. For example, during the worst years of the depression, the packers used their economic power to pass along to the rancher any drop in prices. As a result, while many Argentine ranchers went to the wall, the packing houses continued to take average earnings of 10 to 15 per cent.

Next, the packers' products are sold all over the world. As William told the Royal Commission – 'You kill an animal in one country and the product of that animal is sold in fifty different countries.' For taxation purposes, this raises the vital question, where is the profit made? If, like the Vesteys, you own not only the packing houses, but the ranches that raise the cattle, not only the freezing works that store the carcases but the refrigerated ships that carry them abroad, not only the docks that unload them, but the companies that insure them, not only the wholesalers that distribute them, but the butchers who sell them, then you can take your profit at the most convenient stage down this line. The most convenient stage is naturally where you will pay the least taxation, preferably where you will pay none at all.

In 1919 the major part of the Vestey empire was located abroad. The Vesteys could have taken their profits in any one of a dozen or more countries. They could have returned to Argentina, had the profits sent to them there, and have paid no income tax at all. But they wanted to live in Britain. They were tired of exile. Given this, the problem they faced was how to get the money they needed for their personal living expenses into Britain and yet pay no tax on it. The number of people who have solved this problem for any length of time must be small: witness the number of pop singers, film stars, and successful authors who have gone protesting into tax exile and have had to stay there. But the Vesteys had, back in 1919, a head start. In Edward Brown, William's personal secretary, they had one of the most brilliant accounting brains of the day. Brown evolved the scheme that for sixty years has thwarted the best that the Inland Revenue has been able to throw at it. Brown entered the Revenue's mind, perceiving not only paths through the current tax legislation but anticipating what later generations of Revenue officers might do in order to bring the Vesteys into the tax net. His scheme, with its intricate subtleties, required many pages of legal jargon to explain, but its main thrust can be readily understood.

First, the Vesteys had to go abroad again, in case by remaining in Britain they re-established residence. From July, 1919 until September, 1920, they lived in Holland, and from then until April, 1921 in Hamburg. When they left they had not expected to be away quite so long, but it took Brown, solicitors, and tax counsel more than two years to finalise the scheme. Edmund arrived back in Britain on April 12, 1921 and William on April 23. They took furnished houses – it would have been legally unwise to have bought a residence – and on December 29 and 30 that same year put their signatures to documents that were to make legal and taxation history.

The actual signing took place abroad. The Vesteys first went to Brussels where, at 39 rue Ernest Allard, they leased the greater part of their overseas empire to their British company, Union Cold Storage Ltd. The lease said that for twenty-one years from April 10, 1921, Union would pay a rent of £960,000 (nearly £10 million at today's values) each year for the use of the Vestey cattle ranches, cold storage plants, warehouses, and freezing works, all over the world, from China to Peru. In the normal course of business affairs, the rent paid by Union would have gone to the owners of these valuable properties, the Vestey brothers themselves. But instead the lease provided for Union to pay the rent to three other people: Kenneth Stirling and Charles Auguste Kennerely Hall, both of 4 rue St Anne, Paris, and James Meeres Drabble, of 3 rue Amiral de Joinville, Neuilly sur Seine. Hall and Stirling were both lawyers, and Drabble was a company director. Hall came from an old Liverpool family; all three were well-known to the Vesteys, were fully trusted, and were well rewarded for what they were required to do.

The next day, at the Paris offices of Hall and Stirling, the Vesteys signed a deed of settlement, or a family trust document. The deed began with the usual explanation of why it was being created: 'in consideration of the natural love and affection of the settlors for the beneficiaries hereafter referred to, and for divers other good causes and considerations.' The deed then went on to set out what would happen to the £960,000 a year rent. It was to be held in a 'settled fund' and then invested by the trustees. The income that these investments produced was to be divided into two parts, half going to 'William's Fund', half to 'Edmund's Fund'. These two funds were to be allowed to accumulate for twenty-one years, or until either William or Edmund died, and were then to be used for the benefit of their wives, widows, children, or remoter issue.

At that time, 1921, these payments from William's or Edmund's funds to their relatives could have been made without incurring British tax. (This was later to change.) In this respect the trust was not unusual. It was a straightforward attempt by two rich brothers to protect their wealth from death duties and to set aside some tax-free money for their loved ones. But a crucial factor in such trust arrangements is that the people setting up the trust should not be able to obtain any benefit from it themselves. This did not suit the Vesteys because one of the major reasons for the scheme was to be able to enjoy an income from their business free of tax. So there were other clauses in the settlement deed which enabled them to do just this.

The trustees were given wide powers of investment, including the power to lend on personal credit, or to any company, with or without security. This investment was to be carried out at the direction of certain 'authorised persons'. Who were these authorised persons? None other than William and Edmund Vestey. So what happened was this. The Paris trustees sent large sums of money to the Western United Investment Company in Britain, still the major Vestey holding company today. The trustees entered these payments in their books as 'unsecured loans and advances'. The trustees were fully entitled to do this and Western paid them a commercial rate of interest on the money so advanced.

But Western acted as bankers for the Vesteys and kept personal and property bank accounts for William and Edmund. The Vesteys drew on the personal accounts for private domestic and personal purposes. The property accounts were always in debit; sometimes the personal accounts were in debit, sometimes in credit, but the Vesteys got no interest when they were in the black nor paid any interest when they were in the red. Why should Western, a company with many other shareholders, allow the Vesteys to have bank accounts in the red and charge them no interest? The answer lies in the way Western was incorporated: with one million and four shares of £1 each. The holders of the one million ordinary shares had no rights whatsoever except to receive dividends. The holders of the four management shares had total control of the company and what it did. At the material time the holders of these four vital shares were William, Edmund, and two of their sons. So Western had to do virtually whatever the Vestey brothers wanted. The end result was that as the money flowed into the Paris trust each year – the £960,000 rent and interest from money already invested – large sums flowed out again to Western and from there, tax free, into the pockets of the Vestey brothers.

What did the Inland Revenue think of this? The problem the Revenue faces with overseas trusts is that unless something untoward happens it never learns about them, and even if it does, it is difficult for its investigators to discover much because they have no power to go searching around abroad. The Inland Revenue first learned of the Vestey trust in 1929, eight years after the Vesteys had created it. The circumstances were these. Every year since it had signed the lease with the Vesteys, Union had claimed the £960,000 it paid to the Paris trustees as a tax deduction, arguing that it was one of the costs of operating its business. The Inland Revenue had not queried this until it noticed that in 1922 the sum had been reduced for that one year to £630,000. When it asked about this, Union's answer was to quote a clause from the lease. This said that if at the end of any year Union's profits were not enough to enable it to pay its preference share dividends and to pay at least ten per cent on its ordinary shares, then the rent payable to the Paris trustees would be reduced by as much as was necessary to enable Union to do this.

The Inland Revenue took legal advice on this clause and then rejected Union's tax return. In effect, the Revenue's reply to the clause in the lease was, 'We consider this payment to the Paris trustees is not one necessary to enable Union to *earn* profits, but a payment that *depends* on profits, and, moreover, is payable *out* of profits. It is therefore a sort of dividend and as such is clearly not allowable as a deduction for tax purposes.' Union appealed and won. In 1931 the Revenue took the case to the House of Lords which ruled that the payments were rent and indeed allowable deductions.

But in the course of the case Union was obliged to reveal the existence of the Paris trust and this caused a few raised eyebrows. In the High Court Mr Justice Rowlatt remarked, 'Undoubtedly the relations of this cloud of companies were very complicated; undoubtedly the interests of one family were dominant throughout, and there are very many peculiarities connected with this extensive business.' And in the House of Lords Lord Buckmaster noted, 'It was said that there had been an arrangement of property to avoid payment of income tax, of which, it may be, this document is one of the instruments. But . . . it is admitted that this case has to be determined on the hypothesis that this is a perfectly sound business document.'

So although the Revenue had lost on the issue of the rent, it had achieved something. The veil over the Vestey trust had been lifted a little and the Revenue and the courts had been intrigued by what they had seen. A new Vestey file was opened, and the Revenue began a battle with the Vestey family that was to last for fifty years.

(*See overleaf for illustration of the Paris trust.*)

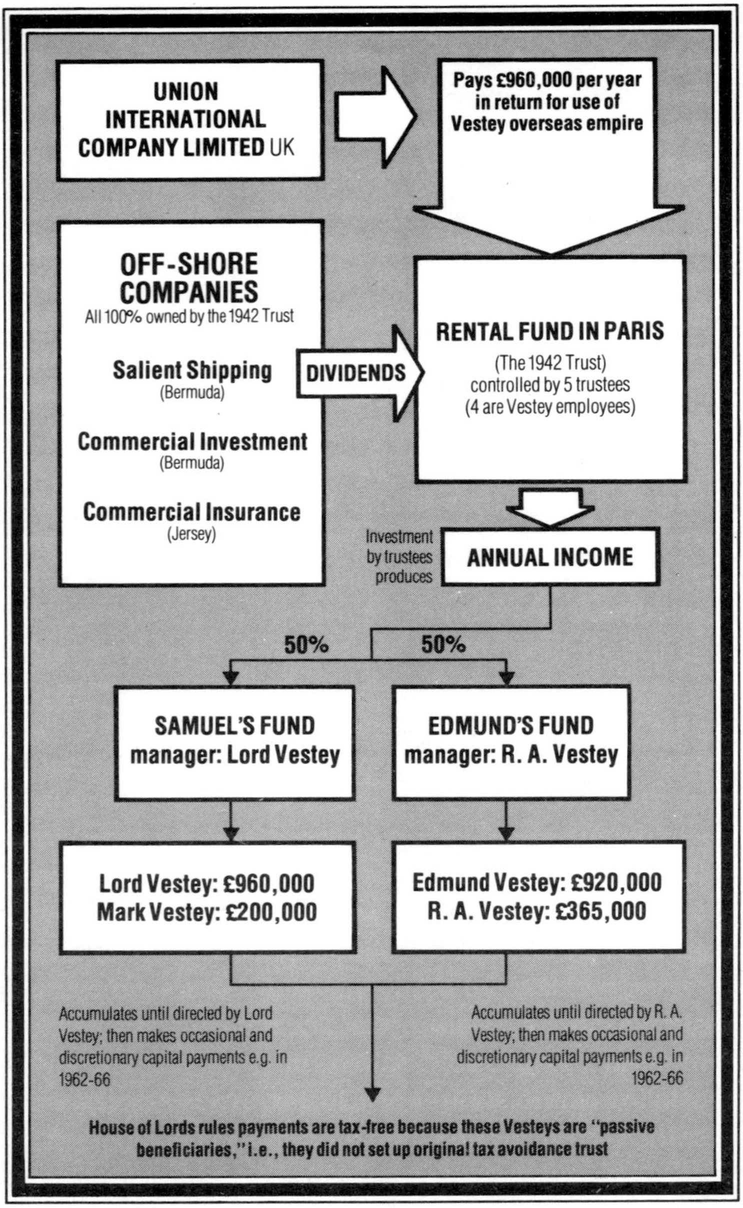
UNION INTERNATIONAL COMPANY LIMITED UK
Pays £960,000 per year in return for use of Vestey overseas empire
OFF-SHORE COMPANIES
All 100% owned by the 1942 Trust
Salient Shipping (Bermuda)
Commercial Investment (Bermuda)
Commercial Insurance (Jersey)
DIVIDENDS
RENTAL FUND IN PARIS
(The 1942 Trust) controlled by 5 trustees (4 are Vestey employees)
Investment by trustees produces
ANNUAL INCOME
50%
50%
SAMUEL'S FUND manager: Lord Vestey
EDMUND'S FUND manager: R. A. Vestey
Lord Vestey: £960,000
Mark Vestey: £200,000
Edmund Vestey: £920,000
R. A. Vestey: £365,000
Accumulates until directed by Lord Vestey; then makes occasional and discretionary capital payments e.g. in 1962-66
Accumulates until directed by R. A. Vestey; then makes occasional and discretionary capital payments e.g. in 1962-66
House of Lords rules payments are tax-free because these Vesteys are "passive beneficiaries," i.e., they did not set up original tax avoidance trust

4

William Buys a Title

King George V is furious

In 1922, William Vestey bought himself a peerage from the Prime Minister, Lloyd George. There was nothing new about the sale of honours in Britain – William Pitt the Younger had said, 'Any man who is master of £10,000 has the right to a Peerage' – but the auction of honours which took place under Lloyd George was on a vast scale. As the historian A. J. P. Taylor writes, 'He ran the system too hard. Not only did he sell more honours with less excuse. Lacking a party, he sold them for his own account.' From a business point of view Lloyd George could not have chosen a better time. There were a lot of men around who had made fortunes during the war and who now had a deep craving for the respectability that a title confers. But the sight of them taking their seats in the Lords upset many. 'Gentlemen received titles whom no decent man would allow in his home,' complained Lt-Col Henry Page Croft in the House of Commons on May 28, 1919. 'And several of them would have been blackballed by any respectable London club.'

How much William Vestey paid to be made a peer is not known. The story in the family is that it cost £25,000. It was gazetted in the Birthday Honours' list on June 22, 1922 and caused something of a stir in the Lords, where among the more conservative members the word went around that William was 'the man who stepped out of cold storage and into the peerage'. But this public criticism was nothing to what went on behind the scenes: a row between King George V and his Prime Minister so bitter that even today the record of it is sparse and hard to find.

The announcement in the *London Gazette* was effusive in listing William's qualities. 'Sir William Vestey, Bart. Managing Director of the Union Cold Storage Company Ltd. Has devoted his life to the production and preservation of food supplies by refrigeration, and has opened up numerous new sources of the supply of refrigerated products from various parts of the world that have materially helped to cheapen the food supply of the people. Rendered immense service during the war to the country and provided gratuitously the cold storage accommodation required for war purposes at Le Havre, Boulogne, and Dunkirk. Head of the Blue Star Line. Has done much relief work for the poor, both in Liverpool and London, and generously contributes to charities.' A later announcement said that William had chosen the title of Baron Vestey of Kingswood (from Kingswood, Dulwich, where he lived.)

The announcement caused immediate resentment. William's evidence to the Royal Commission on Taxation had not gone unnoticed although what he had said had not been widely reported. To make certain that the new peer's views on paying tax were more widely disseminated, Sir Frederick Banbury, Conservative MP for the City of London, considered it his duty to write to the *Morning Post*. Sir Frederick, a master of the quick kill, simply quoted William's evidence and then concluded, 'There does not appear to be any good reason why a person who, during the war, removed his business from this country to avoid taxation, should be made a peer.'

Sir Frederick's letter might have been passed off as a case of sour grapes had not Lord Strachie, a Liberal, raised the matter in the House of Lords where, coincidentally, William had just taken his seat. 'I do not wish to make a personal attack on Lord Vestey,' Strachie said, 'nor do I impute base motives to him. The complaint I want to make is that if the government were aware of the facts I do not see why Lord Vestey should have been recommended for a peerage. This feeling is strong in the country that there should be no awards given to people for avoiding taxation here.' This led Strachie into another sensitive area. 'We have heard a great deal about the sale of honours lately and perhaps Lord Vestey will take this opportunity of assuring this House that neither directly or indirectly did he make any payment for the peerage he received.'

The last thing Lord Vestey wanted to do was to take such an opportunity. He ignored Lord Strachie's invitation altogether and replied only to the accusations about tax. He repeated his plea for his family's need to compete on equal terms with the Americans and the lack of any assurance from the British government that this would be possible. 'I decided to go abroad with the very greatest reluctance,' he said. 'If I had not taken the course I did our new foreign businesses would have had no chance of success. As it was, these works were of very great assistance to the government in providing large quantities of frozen and preserved meat to this and Allied countries, to a large extent from hitherto undeveloped sources.' Earl Stanhope asked whether it was necessary for Vestey to take out foreign naturalisation papers in order to get his business domiciled abroad. Vestey said it was not. Strachie did not press the matter of the purchase of the peerage and there the incident seemed to end.

But, in private, George V took up the question. He did not read the *Morning Post* so he had not seen Sir Frederick Banbury's letter attacking Lord Vestey. But the King did read *The Times*, especially its Parliamentary reports, and when *The Times* of June 30, 1922, duly recorded the exchange in the House of Lords between Strachie and Vestey, the King called for Lord Vestey's evidence before the Royal Commmission on Taxation. What the King read made him very angry indeed. The part of William's evidence that seems to have upset him the most was when, in reply to the question, where are you domiciled at present; in this country? William replied, 'No. Buenos Aires. I am technically abroad at present, but I came over specially to appear before this Commission. The present position of affairs suits me admirably. I am abroad; I pay nothing.' The fact that the Vestey brothers had left Britain in the dark days of 1915 so as to avoid taxation did not strike George V as particularly patriotic and hardly the behaviour expected from a man who had already been honoured by being made a baronet. But that Sir William Vestey, Bt. should say publicly that living in Buenos Aires and paying no tax at all suited him admirably, and that he should then be rewarded with a peerage, brought rushing to the King's pen all the resentment over Lloyd George and his Honours' lists that had been simmering for some time.

So George V sat down and wrote to Lloyd George a letter that in its tone and content must rank among the most critical a British monarch has ever sent his Prime Minister. It is dated from Buckingham Palace, July 3, 1922. It begins 'My dear Prime Minister' (in the King's own hand) and then goes on:

> I cannot conceal from you my profound concern at the very disagreeable situation which has arisen on the question of Honours.
>
> The Peerages which I was advised to confer on Sir J. B. Robinson* and Sir William Vestey have brought things rather to a climax: though for some time there have been evident signs of growing public dissatisfaction on account of the excessive number of honours conferred, the personality of some of the

* Sir J. B. Robinson was one of the mining magnates of the Rand, who, when he died in 1929, left about £20 million. Just before the Honours List was published, it was alleged during a court case in South Africa that between buying a certain mining property and reselling it to his company, Sir J. B. Robinson had made a large and illicit profit for himself. His award caused such an uproar that it was withdrawn. There is a story that the person who had the unpleasant task of telephoning this news to Sir J. B. Robinson, who was old and growing deaf, had some difficulty in making himself understood and that Sir J. B. Robinson, thinking that it was Lloyd George asking for more money, kept repeating, 'But I've already paid.'

recipients, and the questionable circumstances under which the honours in certain instances have been granted.

You will remember that both in conversation and in written communications I have deprecated the ever increasing number of those submitted for the half yearly Honours Gazette, and in recent years there have been instances in which honours have been bestowed where subsequent information has betrayed a lack of care in the enquiries made as to the fitness of the persons selected for recognition.

The case of Sir J. B. Robinson and all that it has evoked in the debates of the House of Lords and in newspaper reports of interviews given by him to Press representatives must be regarded as little less than an insult to the Crown and to the House of Lords and may, I fear, work injury to the Prerogative and the public mind at home and even more in South Africa.

I fully recognise that the inordinate demands upon your time make it impossible for you, in spite of your marvellous capacity for work, personally to investigate the claims and qualifications of those persons whose names you submit for my approval for honours and rewards.

But I do appeal most strongly for the establishment of some efficient and trustworthy procedure in order to protect the Crown and the Government from the possibility of similar painful if not humiliating incidents the recurrence of which must inevitably constitute an evil, dangerous to the social and political well-being of the State.

The letter concluded (again in the King's own hand) 'Believe me, my dear Prime Minister, very sincerely yours, George R.I.'

If Lloyd George was distressed to learn that the King was not only angry at Vestey and Robinson being made peers, but suspected that Lloyd George had sold them the honours, then this distress does not show in his reply. His answer to the King is a mixture of waffle, evasion and lie. He begins, 'I entirely share Your Majesty's concern at the disagreeable situation which has arisen on the question of Honours. No one could feel more strongly than I do the necessity of avoiding any occasion for criticism or complaint in a matter which concerns one of the most important prerogatives of the Crown, and I am most anxious to fulfil Your Majesty's desires for all possible safeguards agains accident or abuse. I deeply regret that such an accident should have occurred in the cases of Sir J. B. Robinson and Sir William Vestey.'

Lloyd George then goes on to defend Robinson saying that he had a long record of great public usefulness in South African industry, was of special service to Britain after the South African War, and had been highly recommended to two previous Prime Ministers, Sir Henry Campbell-Bannerman and Mr Asquith. Lloyd George suggested that Robinson had been a victim of 'capitalistic dislike on account of his sympathies with Labour in South Africa'. He then says, 'With regard to Sir William Vestey, I regret that in this case the evidence which he gave before the Commissioners of Income Tax had not been brought to my notice nor to that of my advisers.'

As for the King's general criticisms, Lloyd George wrote, 'I have recently had occasion to examine the lists which I have had to present to Your Majesty for approval and I do not think it can be said that any of the names which I have suggested for Peerages are not men of distinction and experience in diplomacy, the Army and Navy, Civil Service, Trade, Commerce and Industry. The Lord Chancellor was so much impressed with this series of names that he read them out one by one during the course of the Debate in the House of Lords on Thursday last. I think, also, that the list impressed the Members of the House of Lords who were present. I doubt if any change of system would result in fewer accidents and errors than have marked the Honours Lists of the last seven years. All Ministers and Departments are liable to error and no procedure can be found to avoid all possibility of mistakes.'

The King's criticism about the length of Honours' lists had carried an implied barb: it had suggested that the King knew that his Prime Minister had been selling peerages. But Lloyd George's retort carried the day. 'With regard to the length of recent Honours Lists, I may be permitted to point out that the greater number of Honours conferred in the last few years is due to the enormous burden of the war services borne by the civil population, not one-tenth of which has been, or will ever be, adequately rewarded.'

Lloyd George concluded, 'For my part I entirely share Your Majesty's desire that every possible step shall be taken to protect the Crown and the Government from the possibility of recommendations for Honours being put forward without the most complete justification, and I am now personally engaged with the assistance of my colleagues in considering what further safeguards can properly be taken to that end.'

Our main interest in Lloyd George's letter is his statement about William Vestey: 'I regret that in this case the evidence which he gave before the Commissioners of Income Tax had not been brought to my notice nor to that of my advisers.' Although this may have been literally true – the evidence may not have been brought to Lloyd George's notice – it was a lie in that it implied that Lloyd George did not know the nature of William's evidence when, in fact, he did. For William's evidence closely followed his letter to Lloyd George written in February, 1919, requesting exemption from taxation. In fact, in the exchange in the House of Lords over William's peerage it is interesting to note that the Earl of Crawford did not deny that Lloyd George knew the nature of William's evidence. He used a skilful Parliamentary evasion. 'The evidence which Lord Strachie has summarised was published two years ago, so therefore the Government must be deemed to be technically aware of the substance of it, but I do not think that the Prime Minister has studied it.'

The government was, in fact, greatly embarrassed over the affair because in the Commons the Secretary of State for War, Sir L. Worthington-Evans, was forced to admit that the *London Gazette* announcement of William's peerage contained a serious error. Part of the sentence, 'Rendered immense service during the war to the country and provided gratuitously the cold storage accommodation required for war purposes at Havre, Boulogne, and Dunkirk', was untrue. The Vesteys had not provided all these cold stores free of charge and the government had had to pay.

But once everything was out in the open there was a mild reaction in William's favour. The peers' shock at finding a meat king adding to their numbers soon faded as they noted that the Vestey family appeared to behave in the manner expected. They began by commissioning genealogical research to discover from where the Vesteys had originally sprung. It was not too difficult to go backwards from Samuel – William and Edmund's father – to an earlier Samuel, a wheelwright, who had married an Ann Burrow at Manchester in 1764 and who had died in 1805. But after that, laborious research carried out over a period of forty years failed to establish the origins of this first Samuel. Extensive searches in records of many kinds only showed that the surname, a rare one, was found earlier in certain Leicestershire villages.

An examination of baptismal registers in this area produced only one helpful entry – the baptism of another Samuel, son of William and Alice Vestey, at Sileby on November 27, 1743. Was this the same Samuel Vestey who got married at Manchester in 1764? The Vestey genealogists argued that much research had brought to light no earlier Vesteys in the Manchester area, or indeed, anywhere but in Leicestershire. Searches in the Leicestershire records of later date produced no entry which could refer to the Samuel baptised at Sileby. Therefore, the argument went, if the Sileby Samuel Vestey and the Manchester Samuel Vestey were not one and the same man, then there would have to have been two amazingly mysterious Samuels because one appeared *out* of nowhere and the other vanished *into* nowhere. And then there was the circumstantial evidence of name patterns: the Manchester Samuel had descendants called William, Joseph, Thomas, John, Elizabeth, Alice and Mary, and so did the Sileby Samuel. The evidence was accepted by the examiners at the College of Arms and the Vesteys had the satisfaction of knowing that they came from an old and respectable Leicestershire family.

Next they searched for an ancestral home. Here they

were fortunate. On July 16, 1923, the Earl of Eldon put Stowell Park on the market. Stowell Park, two miles southwest of Northleach, Gloucestershire, had been built in about 1600 for Sir Robert Atkinson, Recorder of Oxford. Set in 6,306 acres with fine views over its park and the river Coln, it was described by the auctioneers as 'one of the finest sporting estates in the country'. The manor house itself consisted of two halls, five reception rooms, sixteen principal bedrooms, twenty-three other bedrooms, five bathrooms, servants' quarters and a badminton court. The estate included eleven farms and numerous small holdings and cottages. The lot was knocked down to an unnamed purchaser for £79,448 including timber. But within two months the sale fell through, and the property was offered at auction again, this time in thirty-two lots. Before the sale could be held, the Vesteys stepped in, and made an offer for the manor house itself and 2,379 acres. The Earl of Eldon accepted the offer and the sale to William's son, the Hon. Samuel Vestey, was completed on September 14, 1923. The purchase price was not revealed, but it was thought to be about £50,000. The Hon. Samuel announced his intention of moving into Stowell Park as soon as certain alterations were made. William decided to stay on at Kingswood, Dulwich, but later also bought that ultimate status symbol of English aristocracy in the twenties, a villa in the south of France.

The Vestey villa was at Menton and William acknowledged the source of the funds that enabled him to acquire it by naming it 'Villa de l'Union', after Union Cold Storage. He spent some of each winter there, but it in no way compared with Kingswood, one of the most unusual town houses in London. Built in 1880, a rambling Victorian mansion in mock Elizabethan style, it had many rooms with marble floors and elaborately-carved panelled walls. But its main feature was its situation. Although it was a *town* house – only half an hour from Union's headquarters in West Smithfield – it was set in 235 acres of lawns and trees, part of the once famous Dulwich Wood, on the side of Sydenham Hill, near Crystal Palace, with a marvellous view over London.

Its previous owners had been two lesser merchant princes, Thomas Tapling, a carpet factor, and John Lawson-Johnson, the man who made 'Bovril' a household name in Britain. The idea of a town house that had such extensive grounds, a long carriage drive bordered by fir trees, and a gate house, appealed to William and he made Lawson-Johnson, a business acquaintance, an offer he could not refuse. The ambitious lad from Liverpool had come a long way. He was rich and getting richer, he was a peer, he had a stately home, a magnificent town house, and a villa in the south of France. All he needed now was to be able to share it with the woman he admired above all others: Evelene Brodstone.

5

The Typist From Nebraska

Evelyn takes control of the empire

Sarah Vestey had been a loyal and faithful wife to William, but in the Victorian manner she had confined herself to bearing his children and running his household; his business neither concerned nor interested her. William accepted this. The idea that a woman could not only be interested in his empire but could run it as well as he could, had – until Evelene Brodstone came along – never occurred to him. Evelene was an American, born in Monroe, Wisconsin, in 1875, the daughter of Hans and Mathilde, poor Norwegian immigrants who later moved to Superior, Nebraska, to farm. When Evelene was seven her father died, and her mother, a dominant figure in Evelene's life, brought her up, struggling to scratch a living from the small Brodstone farm.

Evelene graduated from Superior High School at fourteen, the youngest graduate in the school's history, and then took a course at a business college in Burlington, Iowa. She worked in Superior for a while but the lack of opportunity and her fierce ambition to provide for her mother drove her to Chicago, a move her mother permitted only on the understanding that she stayed with family friends, Mr and Mrs A. S. Briggs, while she looked for a job. In 1895, aged twenty-one, a fair, rather plain girl who used no make-up and favoured simple dresses and cheap cotton stockings, she started work at $12 a week as an office assistant at the Vestey Cold Storage and Packing Company, Chicago. Within twenty years she was to become the world's highest-paid woman executive, the Vesteys' international trouble-shooter, financial confidante, 'mother' of the empire, and, eventually, William's wife.

There are two versions of how Evelene got her start. The one told in her old home town is that Evelene was in the Vestey office one lunchtime – she was sending $8 a week to her mother and could not afford to go out – when William Vestey, in Chicago on a visit, called for a stenographer to take some letters. He was doubtful when Evelene said that there was no one in the office except her but that she would be happy to help. Evelene surprised him with her efficiency and was rapidly promoted. The version within the Vestey family is slightly different. It is that Edmund was running the Chicago office and received one day a letter from William saying he needed an efficient secretary who understood the American end of the business and that Edmund sent him Evelene. The important thing is that within months Evelene was no longer typing letters, but instead acting as minute-taker at directors' meetings, keeping track of Vestey executives on overseas assignments, vetting their reports, and making suggestions for developing the business.

At first the Vesteys tended to resent advice from a woman employee but as Evelene's suggestions usually turned out to be sound, they grew accustomed to consulting her, to allowing her to make decisions in their absence, and then to sending her on assignments overseas. Evelene prepared for these foreign trips with the same dedication she had originally given to shorthand and typing. If she had sufficient notice she studied the language – she ended by being reasonably fluent in twelve. If she had to leave in a hurry she always found time to be briefed by a Vestey employee who had served in the country she was going to visit. She had a flair for figures and a natural feeling for the Vestey business that bordered on intuition. She could read a company report and a balance sheet and not only spot the flaws in the operation but assess its prospects if these were corrected.

Then in 1914, aged forty, comfortable but not well-off, she upset the Vestey brothers by announcing that she was retiring and returning to Superior to spend more time with her mother. She was away barely eight months. The Vesteys decided that they could not handle the extra business that the war would surely bring unless they had Evelene's help. They asked her to return. Evelene drove a hard bargain: she was to be allowed to bring her mother with her at the company's expense. Her mother would live with her in London and accompany her on any overseas trip she wished. And her salary was to be substantially increased. Newspaper reports at the time put the figure at £1,000 a week, but the Vesteys denied this, saying only that she was paid adequately for her services. When the Vestey brothers left for Argentina in 1915, Evelene became even more important. She virtually ran Union in London. They trusted her as if she were family and their consternation can be imagined when Evelene cabled them in 1916 to say that her mother could not tolerate the British climate, her health was suffering, and Evelene was reluctantly taking her back to Superior, Nebraska.

The Vesteys were still considering this bad news when more arrived. The manager of the Hankow packing plant had died suddenly and his deputy, by unfortunate coincidence, was seriously ill. Without direction the whole Chinese operation was in danger of breaking down just when its output was in greatest demand. William acted quickly. He sent Evelene a long cable, one so long that the Superior postmaster complained that it had taken him four hours to receive and transcribe it. Then William caught the first ship out of Buenos Aires and went straight to Superior. It took him three days to convince Evelene to rejoin the Vesteys, this time as their international trouble-shooter. She was to have a contract for five years and a large life annuity as a bonus at the end of the contract period.

Her first assignment was to go to China as fast as possible, and there to find and appoint a new manager. She left immediately via San Francisco and the Pacific and arrived in Hankow in February, 1916. Her work was finished by early March, but then an outbreak of civil war spread to the Hankow district and the Vestey plant and its employees were threatened. Fortunately there was a Blue Star liner loading at the time, and Evelene kept it standing by, steam up day and night, in case she decided to evacuate the Hankow employees. When the danger was over she took the Blue Star steamer to Japan, then a commercial liner to Vladivostock, and then travelled by train across Siberia, Russia and Finland, to London.

The next year saw her in Russia again, this time in Moscow, only two weeks after the Bolshevik Revolution, to try to find out what would happen to the Vestey company there. She arrived on the first train into the city in ten days, sent her luggage to her hotel, and went direct from the station to the Vestey offices. While she was there, a bomb went off in the hotel lobby, destroying Evelene's luggage and killing two hotel porters. She left a week later, the only woman passenger on the train. (The Bolsheviks took over the Vestey plant but the family has a long memory and in 1991 managed to get £1.3 million in compensation for seized assets from both Russia and China.)

The years that followed were Evelene's busiest for the Vesteys. She visited nearly every country in the world. She went to South Africa to track down a Vestey manager who had made off with company funds; she travelled 1,000 miles up the Orinoco River by steamer, then went overland by horseback and packtrain on a nine-week inspection tour of land which the Vesteys had a chance to buy cheaply and which they hoped could be converted to grazing pasture for cattle. She rushed to Australia at short notice to sign a lease of six million acres of cattle land in the Northern Territory. To get there in time she had to travel from Britain to New York by liner, then by a train the Vesteys had chartered to carry Evelene, the only passenger, across the Continent to San Francisco where a Blue Star liner was waiting to take her across the South Pacific to Melbourne.

When the trip was not too risky or too rushed, Evelene took her mother with her. When Mrs Brodstone could not go, Evelene spent as much time between assignments as possible in Superior where she took an active part in public affairs. This interest led to a confrontation with the local council which Evelene handled in a tough but businesslike fashion. The council had wanted to buy some land for a park but it did not have sufficient money. Evelene put up $20,000 which, she said later, was a loan until the council's finances improved. The council claimed that the money was a gift and ignored Evelene's demands for repayment. So she sued them. The pre-trial preliminaries dragged on until the council, faced with a large legal bill and unfavourable publicity, offered to settle. Evelene offered them terms so humiliating that the councillors would certainly have turned them down had not the terms been coupled with others so financially attractive that they could not refuse. The councillors had to acknowledge publicly that they had been wrong and had tried to keep $20,000 that was not rightfully theirs. In return for this apology, Evelene agreed to allow the council to keep the $20,000 to which she would add whatever amount was necessary to build for the town a new hospital.

In 1921 Evelene's contract with the Vesteys ended and she returned to Superior to live. Two years later, William's wife, Sarah, died. He waited a decent interval and then proposed to Evelene. She accepted, gave a small dinner party for her close friends at Superior – at which she told them nothing of her plans – then went to New York where she met William. On August 9, 1924 they were married at New York's famous 'Little Church Around the Corner'. Evelene was forty-nine, William sixty-five. As one of her wedding gifts to him, Evelene agreed to a long-standing request:

she changed the spelling of her name to the English Evelyn.

In return, William offered to take Evelyn for a honeymoon to any country in the world she cared to name. She chose Ceylon, one of the few places, she said, she had never visited. They were barely installed in their hotel there when a cable arrived from the Vestey offices in London. There had been a fire in the Vestey packing plant in Rio; someone would have to go there to make the insurance claim and supervise rebuilding. Who should it be? Evelyn left for Brazil on the next steamer. William returned to London alone.

The presence of such a powerful personality as Evelyn's in a business that had always been a partnership of two brothers was bound to cause some tension. Until Evelyn arrived, all major decisions had been taken by William and Edmund. Sometimes they would consult Edward Brown, their financial adviser and friend, or Messrs Sing, White and Company, their Liverpool stockbrokers, but basically the two Vesteys steered their empire themselves. When William's respect and admiration for Evelyn's business sense became obvious, Edmund resented it and when William drew Evelyn into the Vesteys' decision-making process this resentment grew into a rift which extended down throughout the organisation. 'You were a William man or an Edmund man,' a former employee recalled, 'and you couldn't change sides and you couldn't be neutral.' William's marriage to Evelyn accentuated the distance between the brothers. William now had an interest outside that of the business. How far the split between the brothers might have developed and how serious might have been its effect on their empire never arose, because in 1924 Edmund, too, fell in love.

He had married young, when he was only twenty-one, an American girl, Sarah Barker, whom he had met when on business in the United States. Since their marriage in 1887 they had had six children. But at fifty-eight, rich, restless, and titled – he had been created a baronet in 1921 – he met Ellen Soward, who lived not far from Edmund's home in Shirley, Croydon. Lady Vestey filed a petition for judicial separation, alleging acts of cruelty, and her case came before a judge and special jury in July, 1924. The granting of a judicial separation in those days placed an obligation on the husband to support the wife in the manner to which she had become accustomed. So Lady Vestey's lawyers called her to give evidence of her life-style and her husband's income.

In the course of this evidence she electrified the court and horrified Edmund by saying that her husband's income was at least £150,000 a year. This came as something of a surprise to the Inland Revenue to whom Edmund had been declaring a comparatively modest income, largely from directors' fees. Further evidence on his means and demands for documents or account books might well involve disclosing the whole story of the Paris trust, something both the Vestey brothers wanted to avoid at all cost. So the case suddenly stopped short, and some out-of-court negotiation replaced the court hearing. At the end of this negotiation, Edmund wrote his wife a remarkable letter.

'My dear Sarah. – I regret it is not possible for us to live together again and I wish you to take this as final. In the month of September, 1922, I stayed for several days at the Hotel Normandy, Deauville, under the name of

Mr Allerton, accompanied by a lady, occupying the same bedroom, and again, from Friday the 22nd to Sunday, the 24th of this month, under the name of Mr Douglas, I stayed at the Royal Palace Hotel, Ostend, with the same lady, both occupying room 331. The hall porter and other members of the staff will have no difficulty in recognising me. – Yours sincerely, E. H. Vestey.'

Naturally Edmund had not provided his wife with such a convenient confession of his adultery without the expectation of something in return, namely that she would sue him for divorce. Equally, Lady Vestey would have agreed to this course only if she felt that arrangements for her financial needs would be catered for. But there were still some last-minute negotiations to be conducted. Lady Vestey initiated enquiries to confirm for her proposed action the truth of what Edmund had told her in his letter. Surprisingly, the enquiries were, she wrote to him, 'ineffectual' and therefore she proposed to take no action in the matter. There were further meetings between lawyers acting for the two and on October 29, 1923, Edmund wrote to his wife again saying that he had made a mistake in his previous letter: the name he had used at Deauville was Allison, not Allerton. This time Lady Vestey's enquiries were successful, Lady Vestey filed for divorce and the divorce court judge awarded her a decree nisi with costs.

The decree was made absolute on March 8, 1926. Two days later Edmund and Ellen Soward were married at the Princes-row Register Office, Buckingham Palace Road. The divorce and the marriage made a few paragraphs in the newspapers and were forgotten, except by the Inland Revenue, where the court report that Edmund's income was £150,000 a year was carefully clipped and filed.

*

William Vestey, when he was not travelling, lived quietly with his new bride in Dulwich. William's son, Samuel, lived in some splendour in Stowell Park, Gloucestershire. Edmund now felt that he needed a residence befitting his status and suitable for *his* new wife. So he built a palace in Kent. He told the architect, Sir Charles Allom, to spend as much as he liked. In the end the house cost £225,000 in 1927 (£3.1 million at today's values) and became known as 'the only residence on the south coast fit for Royalty'. It was built on a ten-acre site on the North Foreland at Broadstairs with a fine view of the sea and with a private entrance to a bathing beach. A colonnade ran along the south and east sides and all the second-floor rooms opened on to a verandah supported by the colonnade. The drawing-room and the library, panelled with classic ornamentation picked out in gilt, overlooked the sea, and a courtyard opened on to the gardens with their lily ponds, fountains, and a large ornamental pool spanned by a bridge in Japanese style. Stone balustrade walls marked the end of each terrace and there was an orchard, a vineyard, a summer house, a tennis court and a timber pavilion for deck quoits. The five principal bedrooms were arranged in suites, each with its own bathroom lined with the finest Italian marble. There was a gatekeeper's lodge with five rooms, a chauffeur's cottage, and accommodation for up to ten household staff. As a last-minute addition, the architect included a built-in organ in the hall.

Edmund later regretted spending so much money on what the locals called 'The Meat King's Folly'. At the time he justified it as his only extravagance, the reward of a man who had worked hard all his life and now, with a new wife, deserved a little luxury. Besides, he said, it was a good investment. At West Smithfield, however, the staff of Union called it 'keeping up with William'.

6

The Vestey Style

The curious case of the fake corned beef

By the mid-twenties the laissez-faire attitude that had enabled the Vesteys to establish and consolidate their fortune was beginning to disappear. The primary producing countries of the world had started to resent what they saw as exploitation by the big companies from consumer nations. At first their demands were modest – a larger slice of the profit for the rancher – but they became more ambitious: why could they not do themselves what the foreign company did? As far as William and Edmund were concerned, the rot had set in with the Bolshevik revolution, when the President of the Supreme Council of the Soviet Union's National Economy had nationalised the Russian branch of Union Cold Storage and handed all its stores, railway sidings, and packing plants to the Food Department of the Moscow Soviet. In China, riots and civil war were making business difficult and in Argentina a growing sense of nationalism coupled with worker discontent at low wages and poor conditions in foreign meat packing plants caused almost constant conflict.

The Vesteys had not become millionaires by allowing difficulties like these to stand in the way of making a profit. They were ingenious, unorthodox and, in the old days, quick to reach for the law and, if possible, for help from their government, when anyone got in their way. They were firm believers in maintaining what, in advertising or public relations jargon, would be termed 'their image'. They knew that they had a reputation as hard, tough businessmen from whom no one got a penny more than his due and they took a lot of trouble to maintain this reputation. One example gives the flavour of the Vestey approach to business. In the early thirties a shipment of frozen egg from China arrived in Liverpool in a spoiled condition. The Vesteys had taken the trouble to insure the cargo with Lloyds and they duly claimed. The amount was disputed, but eventually the Lloyds syndicate settled for payment of £14,000. The Vesteys collected £13,978 – one small underwriter had refused to contribute his £22 share of the claim. The Vesteys sued him, engaged counsel, took the matter before the King's Bench Division of the High Court, and then, at the last minute, accepted his offer of £11.

The underwriter had experienced on a small scale what the Vesteys were like internationally, and there is no better way to show this than to take a series of incidents in the twenties and thirties when times were hard, but the Vesteys were harder. We begin with what became known as the Great Meat War.

In 1922 the Vestey brothers bought the British and Argentine Meat Company, a thriving meat packer and exporter with plant in Argentina and considerable assets in

Britain. With their modern works at South Dock, Buenos Aires, well under way, the Vesteys wanted to consolidate their share of the Argentine meat trade. This was a matter of negotiation, not with the Argentine ranchers, or even the Argentine government, but with the other packers. For the packers had long ago formed a cartel, which they called a conference, and this conference allocated to its members a fixed proportion of the total amount of meat exported from Argentina to the markets of the United States, Britain, and Europe. The Vesteys had joined the conference in June, 1922 when, as was customary, the quotas of the smaller packers were cut to provide a share for the newcomer.

The Vesteys now attempted to dominate the conference. They quickly leased one of their plants to another company, the River Plate, British and Continental Meat Company, and entered into an agreement with that company to act as its selling agents in Britain and Ireland. The Vesteys then proposed that this new firm be given a conference quota by reducing the quota of all other plants – except the Vesteys' because, they claimed, the American company Swift was building a new plant at Rosario and if the British were to hold their own against the Americans, then the Vesteys would have to keep their full quota. The smaller British firms objected, pointing out that the proposal meant that the Vesteys would not merely keep their quota but increase it, because they were acting as selling agents for the new company. The chairman of one of the small British companies said, 'The Vesteys want the biggest slice of a cake that is already too small.' The issue was brought to a head by a growing disagreement between the larger companies and in April, 1925, the conference was suspended.

The conference had enforced its quotas by witholding shipping space from any company which tried to break away. In the free-for-all that followed the end of the conference, the Vesteys were well placed because they owned a shipping line, Blue Star, with extensive refrigerated capacity. They began to buy heavily, ship to Britain, and flood the market with cut-price meat. The American companies responded, determined to teach the Vesteys a lesson and establish their dominance of the market as they had done in an earlier price war in 1913.

But the industry had come a long way from the days of 1913, and there was no comparison between the rivals the Americans faced then and those they faced in 1925. The Vesteys, who led the battle against the Americans, were now the owners of the largest group of multiple butcher's shops in Britain. They had grown into the world's largest retailers of meat, owned one third of Britain's cold storage space, and in Blue Star, had one of the world's largest fleets of refrigerated ships. This was a real competitor as the Americans quickly learnt. Down and down went the price of meat until some cuts were selling at Smithfield at less than three halfpence a pound (less than 1p). Throughout this battle, the Vesteys flew from their Smithfield headquarters a huge Union Jack as if to suggest that they were fighting a patriotic struggle for the good of the housewives of Britain. It was, of course, no such thing.

For a start, although the housewife benefited from reduced meat prices during the battle, this was never more than a temporary measure. Once the big packers had settled their differences and divided the largest slice of the cake between them the battle was no longer between the Vesteys on one side and Swift and Armour on the other, that is between Britain and America. For the small packers, left with a share of the market they felt was not large enough to ensure their existence, continued the battle; but now it was the Vesteys with Swift and Armour on one side and the small packers on the other. And the most bitter battle was between the Vesteys and the Smithfield and Argentine Meat Company, both British firms, the Vesteys blaming Smithfield and Argentine for holding out against a restoration of peace in the industry and Smithfield and Argentine blaming the Vesteys for having started the trouble in the first place.

So the real losers were the small packing houses who did not have the resources to stand the losses which the price war made inevitable, and – in the long run – the Argentine ranchers who had to accept the price offered to them by the cartel (or the big packers when the cartel was in disarray) or not sell their cattle at all. The meat war was not the battle for freedom of trade and choice, as the Vesteys tried to present it, but an internal quarrel between the giants of the business as to how they should divide the spoils of their monopoly.

It was inevitable that the rise of nationalism in Argentina would eventually oblige the government there to look more closely at the operations of the foreign meat packers and their cartel. The packers wielded considerable political clout and it was not until 1934 that a group of Argentine senators managed to get government backing for an investigating committee to look into the ownership of the packing houses, their profit levels, the workings of their cartel and their labour practices. One of the first packing houses the committee looked at was the Vesteys and the senators called the local Vestey manager, Richard Tootell, before them to examine him.

Tootell began his evidence with a statement of principle. He said that the Vesteys were prepared to co-operate with the committee and would discuss with it everything *except* production costs. Since these figures were vital for the committee's work, the chairman, Senator Lisandro de la Torre, asked Tootell to reconsider his attitude and when Tootell refused, surprised everyone by placing Tootell under arrest for contempt. Tootell pleaded that he had not intended contempt, but that the information the committee required was not in Argentina, but in London, and had been sent there earlier at London's request.

Unfortunately for the Vesteys, the next day de la Torre received an anonymous tip that a Vestey ship, the *Norman Star*, was about to sail for London with a suspicious cargo on board. De la Torre had the coastguard detain the ship and the customs search it. In one hold, under a cargo of foul-smelling guano, the Argentine customs officers found twenty-one cases labelled 'corned beef', sealed with the seals of the Argentine Ministry of Agriculture. The ship's captain was unable to explain why corned beef was being carried hidden in bird-droppings, so the customs officers removed the crates for proper examination.

Broken open on the dockside, the crates were found to contain not corned beef, but Vestey company documents: payrolls, balance sheets, internal memoranda, cables, and company minutes. The committee seized them, and Tootell, who was about to be released on bail, was kept under technical arrest. In London, William immediately protested to the Foreign Office, where his reception was somewhat chilly. 'Vesteys' actions in this matter have by no means been entirely above board,' wrote one Foreign

Office official. 'We ourselves have had many reasons for complaint against them in the past.' So the Foreign Office confined itself to making certain that Tootell was properly treated and when more Vestey documents were found in Uruguay, the Foreign Office felt that it had to agree to the Argentine government's request to make de la Torre's committee of enquiry a joint governmental one. This meant that the committee would be able to examine the operations of the meat packers in Britain as well as in Argentina.

William immediately saw the danger. Such a committee would want to inspect the Vestey books in London, and there was no telling what such a probe might uncover, particularly about the Vestey trust and its elaborate arrangements to avoid tax. He resisted with all his considerable power. In the time it had taken to set up the joint committee Tootell had returned to London where, aged only fifty-one, he collapsed and died. William lost no time in accusing Senator de la Torre of Tootell's murder. He wrote to the committee a long rambling letter saying that de la Torre was using the Vesteys as a 'political football' to defeat the ruling party in Argentina by arousing the people's passions against foreign-owned meat packing plants.

'There is not the slightest doubt that he was responsible for what turned out in fact to be the murder of our general manager, Richard Tootell,' William wrote. 'Mr Tootell recently fell dead at only fifty-one years of age (leaving his widow not in good health to go through the remainder of her life alone) through injury done to his health by Senator de la Torre's deliberately insulting and aggravating attitude towards Mr Tootell personally during his examination, and then ordering his being put into gaol and kept under arrest. This resulted in the complete breakdown of Mr Tootell's health, so that Senator de la Torre's committee were compelled to allow him to come home to England on bail for fear of his dying on their hands.'

The Argentine government hit back. At an official level they wrote to the Foreign Office saying that Vestey's letter 'constitutes an unprecedented piece of insolence – there is no other word for it in our language – to the British and the Argentine governments.' It asked that William be prosecuted for criminal libel. Unofficially, Dr Evaristo Uriburu, a former ambassador to London, made a point of seeking out members of the British embassy in Buenos Aires and telling them that the Vesteys were 'unscrupulous', and had 'disgraced the good name of England'. Uriburu, a cattle breeder, said that he had had unsatisfactory business dealings with the Vesteys as had several of his friends and their 'bad reputation' was no more than they deserved.

All Dr Uriburu's comments were, of course, passed back to the Foreign Office. In one letter, dated May 15, 1935, the embassy reported, 'Dr Uriburu referred also to the reputation of the Vesteys in England, mentioning that Lord Vestey was known to have obtained his peerage by contributing £20,000 to party funds, and describing his cold reception by the House of Lords, not omitting the comment that was then made that his elevation to the peerage was a disgrace to the House. All this, no doubt, Dr Uriburu has imparted to his friends in the Government, and the firm's treatment of so influential a person – at no great pecuniary advantage to themselves, for the amounts in question were quite small – illustrates how mistaken their tactics have been.'

When the Foreign Office replied that in English law there was no case against William for criminal libel, and although William's letter was 'certainly offensive' it did not see what it could do about it, the work of the Joint Committee of Enquiry was effectively emasculated. Word of the Foreign Office's attitude may have leaked to William because he made an impassioned plea to be exempt from the Joint Committee's enquiries. 'After all this ill-treatment of our British works in which millions of pounds of British capital are invested, distributing meat to some millions of the poorer people of Britain each week through our company's 2,500 retails shops established during the last fifty years, the Joint Committee, in common justice for the brutal manner in which the Senate enquiry was conducted, should absolve us from anything further to do with this enquiry.'

It worked. The committee went on for more than two years, and held sixty meetings, and although its report in 1938 was considered a landmark in the history of the Argentine meat trade, it never did get to see the Vestey books. Senator de la Torre, the man who had come nearer than anyone else to penetrating the secrecy of the Vestey empire, shot himself on January 5, 1939, leaving a suicide note which expressed his disappointment at the general behaviour of mankind.

By 1933 Britain was suffering heavily from the worldwide depression. Inflation, as measured by the annual index of prices of consumer goods and services, not only stopped, it turned into deflation. Millions were unemployed and the financial world was in a state of jitters. Even the Vesteys began to find the going tough: when Union Cold Storage came to make up its accounts in July, 1933, it found that after paying its preference share dividends and ten per cent of its ordinary shares, there was not sufficient money left to make the full annual rental payment to the Paris trustees. They had to be content with half, because – as the case brought by Inland Revenue had highlighted – the lease between Union and the Paris trustees provided for a reduction in the rent if Union's profits were not sufficient to meet its dividend obligations.

So the Vestey family found itself hit from two directions. If there were any reduction in the rent going to the Paris trust, the trustees would have less money to invest and accumulate for the Vesteys. Union had paid its ordinary shareholders a ten per cent dividend for the past thirty-two years. Now that times were hard, it could have argued that it would be justified in reducing this ten per cent. Such a reduction would leave more money to pay the Paris trustees. But reducing this dividend to the ordinary shareholders of Union would hit the Vesteys just as much as reducing the £960,000 rent because the entire ordinary shareholding of Union belonged – under various names – to the Vesteys themselves.

William and Edmund decided, therefore, that the only thing to do was to cut dividends to the only other shareholders left – those holding Union's preference shares. This audacious proposal produced some of the wildest scenes ever seen in the City, the almost unanimous condemnation of the British financial establishment – *The Times* said it undermined the whole basis of contractual relations – and a court case in which more details of the Vesteys' tax arrangements emerged.

The proposal was this: Union had an issued capital of £12 million. Only £1 million of this was ordinary stock and £11 million was in preference shares – £8 million at six per cent, £2 million at seven per cent, and £1 million at ten per cent. The Vesteys proposed to reduce the six per cent shares to five per cent, the seven per cent shares to six per cent and the ten per cent shares to seven per cent. Since the whole point of a preference share is that it is a contract to pay a dividend at a fixed percentage, even the Vesteys did not expect to get away with reducing the percentage without some compensation. They offered an immediate payment of 2*s* a share to make up for the loss, and said that they proposed to call a meeting in a week's time to learn the shareholders' decision.

Even before the peculiarities of the proposal emerged there was strong opposition. London, Glasgow and Liverpool stock exchanges protested and invited the council of the Association of Stock Exchanges to act 'in this latest case of attempted interference with shareholders' rights and privileges', and in the general interest of financial business. A joint committee of the British Insurance Association and the Association of Investment Trusts examined the Vestey proposal and recommended against acceptance. (What worried the institutional investors was that as the depression forced interest rates down companies would try to replace dear loans with cheaper loans and the Vestey proposal would be a dangerous precedent.)

The preference shareholders' meeting on November 29, 1933 was filled to overflowing. As *The Times* said, 'Not for many years has so much interest been taken by the investing public, professional and private, as in the "unique" – to use the official description – project of Union Cold Storage which was discussed at largely attended meetings held yesterday to consider it.' Before the meeting ended in uproar the preference shareholders managed to get more information from the Union officials. The Vesteys considered that the move was necessary to safeguard the future of the company which could be in doubt because of 'difficult trading due to quotas and restrictions of various kinds'. The reduction in interest rates would save the company about £130,000 a year. The cost of the compensation to the preference shareholders would be about £1.3 million. It was correct to say, therefore, that the company would be obtaining a ten per cent investment on a capital outlay of £1.3 million. But where was the £1.3 million coming from? This proved hard to discover. At the meeting all that Union officials would say was that it would not be made out of the resources of the company 'but on behalf of the ordinary stockbrokers'. It was not until the affair ended in the High Court that the reason for this reticence emerged.

When the meeting degenerated into what *The Times*' financial editor described as 'unprecedented scenes' the company tried to take a poll. But there were not sufficient ballot boxes, no tables to hold them, and not enough people to collect them. Afterwards some disgruntled stockholders met in a nearby hotel room and formed a stockholders' committee to oppose the company's scheme. This proved a wise move because on December 7, the company announced that the polls had shown that the required majority of shareholders had accepted the company's offer and that it would be implementing it as soon as possible. *The Times*, in reporting the poll result, suggested in a restrained comment that the poll returns were remarkably low: Of the six per cent shareholders, only 46.8 per cent had voted; of the seven per cent, only 43.1 per cent; and of the ten per cent, only 17.8 per cent.

The shareholders' committee moved swiftly. George Edward Hughes, a solicitor, acting on behalf of himself and others, obtained an injunction restraining Union from going ahead. The Vesteys contested the injunction and the full hearing of the case began in the High Court on July 9, 1934 and lasted six days. Counsel for Hughes had been very busy in the interim and had come up with some interesting answers to the questions Union Officials had dodged at the shareholders' meeting the previous year. The £1.3 million to pay off the preference shareholders was to come from the Western United Investment Company which held all the ordinary shares in Union. But who owned Western United? The Vesteys owned the four management shares and the one million ordinary shares were owned by the Paris trust, set up by the Vesteys for the benefit of the Vesteys.

So William and Edmund's whole scheme came tumbling out. By lowering the dividends to Union's stockholders, the Paris trust would have a better chance of getting its full £960,000 rent out of Union. But Union could not substantially lower its dividend to the ordinary shareholders of Union because the ordinary shares were all held by the Paris trust. So the only group left to squeeze were the preference shareholders. Union admitted that it had not told the preference shareholders these intriguing details in its circular proposing the deal, and the Stock Exchange Committee members gave evidence that they considered Union's offer to be inequitable: 'If the principle is accepted then the effect on many millions of pounds of invested capital will be very serious indeed.'

After that Mr Justice Eve had no hesitation in saying that the votes of the stockholders had been cast on 'a wholly inadequate disclosure of material facts'. He said that the Vesteys should have revealed to the preference stockholders the details of Union's lease arrangements with the Paris trustees. The stockholders, represented by George Hughes, were entitled to their injunction and their costs.

In March, 1927, riots and civil commotion in Nanking wrecked the Vestey packing plant, warehouses, and offices. A joint Chinese–British Commission assessed the total damage in what became known as the Nanking Incident at $2,318,023 of which $1,334,120 represented compensation for the Vestey losses. The Chinese government agreed to pay the compensation as soon as it could, and up to February, 1929 made two payments totalling $300,000, most of which went to the widows of three British subjects who had been killed during the fighting. In June, 1930, the Chinese government made a further payment of $100,000. There was then a gap of over a year because the civil war and the financial situation made it impossible for the government to pay. In 1931, as a result of vigorous and repeated representations from the British government, China began to pay $100,000 a month, and in February, 1935 the Vesteys received the last instalment of the $1.3 million due to them. But they were not happy.

'We have today received a cable from our people in Nanking advising that they have received the final instalment,' wrote the Hon. Samuel Vestey, William's son, who was now taking over the day-to-day running of the business, in a letter of complaint to the Foreign Office. 'In their cable they mention that the British Consulate has requested them to sign a receipt which reads "in final settlement". We have requested them not to sign this receipt for the present as there is still the question of interest to be settled with the Chinese authorities.' Taking this at an average of six per cent from the time the claim was made until it was finally paid meant that the Chinese government still owed the Vesteys a further $320,823.26, Samuel wrote. 'We shall be obliged if the Foreign Office will ask your people in China to present this claim for us and to press for payment as early as possible.'

The Foreign Office was indignant: 'It is only with the utmost difficulty that we have persuaded the Chinese government to pay something towards the loss caused to His Majesty's government by the depreciation of the Shanghai dollar,' wrote one official. 'It is in the highest degree unlikely that they would entertain for one moment a claim for interest, and they could point, I think with reason, to the fact that the question of interest was always waived when it cropped up.' But the Foreign Office had not become skilled in diplomacy for nothing. It submitted the Vestey claim to the Chinese nevertheless, 'in order that they may bear the odium of refusing to ask for it.' Letters were still going back and forth, with the Vesteys steadfastly refusing to drop their claim, when the war made the whole matter irrelevant.

Although the Vestey operation in Russia had been nationalised when the Bolsheviks came to power, the Vesteys succeeded in hanging on there until the thirties, a demonstration of their conviction that trade transcends political persuasion, people have to eat and governments that do not feed them do not last long. Their approach to the Soviet government was simple: if you want to sell your produce, we'll buy; if you want to buy our produce, we'll sell. On this basis a deal was done. The Vesteys sent the Soviet government margarine and fats from Argentina at any time of the year on credit. When the Russian butter season arrived, the Soviet government repaid the Vesteys with big shipments of butter, sent direct to Britain.

It was a neat deal but not without its hiccups. Every now and then a zealous Communist Party official would want to know what the Soviet Union was doing trading with the capitalist Vesteys, and why the Union Cold Storage company, nationalised in 1919, was still in business in Russia. There would be a purge and the Vesteys would be accused of all sorts of crimes. In 1930, for example, the Soviet authorities executed forty-eight people for 'conspiracy to defeat the Soviet food plans', and named the Vestey man in Moscow, a Mr Fothergill, as being involved in the conspiracy.

Fothergill, the Russians said, had offered a bribe of £10,000 to Professor Riazantsev, an employee of the Soviet department controlling cold stores and warehouses. The Vesteys denied this and rushed to the British Foreign Office to arrange an official protest. They were concerned, they said, about the fate of Mr Fothergill. They were also determined not to let the Soviet charges pass without protest because, as the Foreign Office cynically noted, 'the Soviet Government owes them over £500,000 and the company remains suspicious that the accusations may have been made in order to provide an excuse for not paying this money when it falls due.' The Vesteys got their money, but their days in Russia were numbered.

By the thirties the Vestey operation was so well integrated that not only could the family keep all the profits to themselves, they could also control the market to increase those profits. If you own every link in the chain between meat producer and meat consumer you can use the power that this gives you to squeeze out opposition, fix your own prices, and take your profit where you will. The Vesteys' competitors could not complain about this. For one thing, the meat business being what it is, they would no doubt have done the same themselves if they had been able. But occasionally someone who knew enough about the trade to realise what the Vesteys were up to – but who was not directly involved – felt a duty to speak out. One such person was the Duke of Atholl, one of Scotland's leading dukes.

The Duke was also a director of Bovril, the meat extract company, but this was not the reason for his protest. In fact, the Vesteys had improved Bovril's profits by keeping meat prices down. The Duke said that he made his protest to protect British interests in Argentina where he felt that the Vesteys' greed was endangering not only their own operation but that of all British business. So on August 16, 1932, the Duke wrote a long letter to the Prime Minister, Ramsay MacDonald, most of which concerned the Vesteys. It is worth quoting large parts of it because of the light it throws on Vestey methods, both in Argentina and in Britain.

'At the present moment the Argentine has an enormous amount of cattle,' the Duke began. 'This is owing partly to bad prices and to a great extent to the action of the Vestey Combine. Vestey had got control – or almost complete control – of the meat market. The owners of the cold storage establishments join together in a ring, the two most powerful being Vestey and Swift. It was decided that each should have a quota for himself. Vestey then bought up the smaller ones and has ended in having nearly all the quotas himself, and thus controls the organisation. He holds the British market.

'This combine, being only sellers, crashed prices in the Argentine to the producers, and cattle are being produced at a dead loss, and large numbers of producers, who are many of them quite small people, will go to the wall. Vestey does not produce, but purchases. The animals then go to his plant. The by-products – although he squeals a lot about the price of hides – pay not only the price at which he buys, but also for the freight to England. He brings meat in his own ships to Smithfield, where he again controls the price, and keeps it as low as possible. This crashes the price for his competitors on the wholesale market, and he purchases their meat at his crashed price.

'He controls or owns an enormous quantity of meat shops in England and is becoming almost a monopoly, so that if you mention his name near a meat market people look over their shoulders. The meat is sold to their retailers, a great many of whom are really his own shops or are controlled by him in various names, and he takes 15 to 20 per cent profit. He charges high prices to the retailer in places like Brighton, where there is no competition, but he is prepared to cut his price in the London market if anybody should show their nose.

'The retailers of course can charge anything they like over and above the price that he charges them. They are another line of business, though generally himself, but I should think that probably for income and super-tax purposes they are treated separately. The real point is that he is getting far too big a profit. The retail price is not necessarily too high, but some of his profit ought to go to the producers. Vestey . . . scoops a great deal of money out of the Argentine. And it is certainly a problem which has got to be dealt with.'

Atholl's letter went the rounds of Whitehall but nothing happened. He need not have worried too much about the Argentine ranchers because the Vesteys' own actions in Argentina brought about their downfall there, as in Russia and, eventually, China, thus closing to them the three countries that had made their original fortune.

7

The Taxman Fails

The Vesteys keep their millions

The Second World War began badly for the Vesteys. When France was over-run there was some fighting near Menton and their villa was shelled. It took some time for the news to reach London, but eventually their agent in Marseilles got word to William that the villa had been 'devastated'. Evelyn was particularly distressed – 'We've had some very happy times there,' she wrote to friends in the United States, 'and no one knows whether they'll ever come again.' Then when the blitz began, Kingswood, the Vesteys' London house, was nearly hit by a parachute mine. It landed in the grounds, but the concussion blew out all the windows, brought down walls and mirrors, and lifted the marble floors. William felt that the air raid shelter in the wine cellar was no longer sufficient protection and after some hunting around for a suitable place outside London he took Evelyn to a house in Bull Lane, Gerrards Cross. His son, Samuel, found accommodation nearby and the two of them would go up to the Smithfield offices by car.

There the news seemed always to be bad. Evelyn summed it up: 'William has just come in this minute from the office with news that our last new boat has been sunk, fully-loaded and nearly home. Damn Hitler . . . We surely seem to be having terrific losses. Our losses are more for our particular kind of ship than all the other lines who have similar ships put together. The last four ships cost almost fifteen million dollars, but no money can ever replace our dear *Arandora Star* and her captain and his men.'* William's health was failing and the loss of this ship was a double blow to him. For some time he had been taking what he called 'electrical treatment' from an Italian doctor living in London. The Italian had been interned in the round-up of aliens soon after the outbreak of war and was on the *Arandora Star*. He survived but William had lost his services.

As William grew more feeble, the running of the Vestey empire fell more to his brother, Edmund, and his son, Samuel. But Evelyn still had a say. Right up to William's death she was still active, running her own checks on foreign companies that wanted to do business with the Vesteys, and philosophising to friends in the United States on the idle ways of the younger generation. 'If a fat job isn't handed to them on a silver platter they think that the government must provide and no effort is needed on their part.' She was as tough as ever. 'This isn't war, it's just a massacre,' she wrote as the blitz reached its peak in 1940. 'If I were the Powers-that-Be I would give Germany

* The *Arandora Star*, carrying internees to Canada, was torpedoed off the coast of Ireland on July 2, 1940 with the loss of 800 lives.

the same treatment instead of just keeping to military objectives. Force is the only thing they understand and to try to treat the Germans as civilised human beings is just a waste of time. An eye for an eye suits me better than love your enemies.'

William died on December 10, 1940 at Gerrards Cross. He was eighty-one. Almost to the last he continued to be concerned about the evils of taxation and the need to keep his family united against the world. He left only £261,000 in Britain and said in his will that he was making no bequests for charitable purposes because he had given freely in his lifetime and 'the unjust death duties destroy all inclination to give further charitable legacies.' He appointed his sons, Samuel and George, and his friend and confidant, Edward Brown, the man who had devised the Paris trust, as his executors. He charged Samuel, and Samuel's son, William Howarth, to bear in mind that on his death they would become head of the family and that it would be their duty 'to extend good offices and render pecuniary and other assistance to the other members according to their merits and needs'.

William and Edmund had given £220,000 in 1934 towards the building of the great central tower of the Anglican Cathedral at Liverpool, a gift to commemorate their father, Samuel, and their mother, Hannah, and the remains of both parents had been removed from Anfield cemetery and deposited in small caskets at the base of the cathedral tower. William had asked that his remains be buried in the churchyard of the parish church at St Peter Formby, Lancaster, but in 1947 his ashes too were re-interred in the cathedral tower. The obituaries were all laudatory. *The Times* re-told the story of the Vestey rise to riches and added, 'during the last war the vast resources controlled by [his company] were ever at the disposal of the government.'

Evelyn lived only another five months. It had been William and the Vestey empire that had kept her in Britain. Her real home had always been Superior. She went back less after her mother's death in 1924, but the hospital she had endowed became the Brodstone Memorial Hospital, after her mother, and Evelyn continued to take an interest in Superior affairs, never forgetting, for example, to send a gift each Christmas to all the pupils of the first grade at the local school. Now, in accordance with her will, her ashes were returned to Superior and were buried in her mother's grave.

William's death did not go unnoticed at the Inland Revenue. Since the Vesteys' tax arrangements had come to the Revenue's notice they had been waiting for an opportunity to test the validity of the Vesteys' trust in court. But it was not until amendments to the Finance Act in 1936 and 1938 strengthened the Revenue's hand in dealing with overseas trusts that they felt ready to take on the Vesteys. The Treasury had decided that the amendments were necessary in order to deal with the growing use of overseas trusts to avoid British income tax.

What was happening was this: a British resident would transfer some or all of his assets abroad, say to Uruguay. He would appoint a local resident to act as a trustee of those assets. The trustee would invest the assets, collect the income, and then find ways of working that income back to the British resident so that it would not attract income tax – as an occasional, discretionary, capital payment, for example. The introduction to the Finance Act, Section 18, 1936 explains how the Revenue intended to defeat such schemes. It reads, 'For the purpose of preventing the avoiding by individuals ordinarily resident in the United

Kingdom of liability to income tax by means of transfers of assets, by virtue or in consequence whereof, either alone or in conjunction with associated operations, income becomes payable to persons resident or domiciled out of the United Kingdom, it is hereby enacted as follows.'

Then follow ten sub-sections, three of which were added by Section 28 of the Finance Act of 1938. The main one is subsection one, which reads, 'Where such an individual has by means of any such transfer, either alone or in conjunction with associated operations, acquired any rights by virtue of which he has, within the meaning of the section, power to enjoy, whether forthwith or in the future, any income of a person resident or domiciled out of the United Kingdom which, if it were income of that individual received by him in the United Kingdom, would be chargeable to income tax by deduction or otherwise, that income shall, whether it would or would not have been chargeable to income tax apart from the provisions of this section, be deemed to be income of that individual for all the purposes of the Income Tax Acts.'

The sting is in the phrases 'power to enjoy', and 'be deemed to be the income of that individual'. With these, the Inland Revenue believed that they had covered everything. It did not matter now what schemes a tax avoider and his trustees got up to in order to work funds from the offshore trust back to Britain, because the money would be taxable *whether it came back or not*. All the taxman needed to do was to show that the UK resident had the power to enjoy the income of the trustee. Once he had done that he could treat the trustee's income as if it were the income of the UK resident and tax that UK resident accordingly.

A hypothetical example makes the workings of the Act clear. John Doe of Bayswater, London, transfers assets abroad and arranges for the income from those assets to be paid into the John Doe Trust in Uruguay. Doe appoints Juan Lopez as trustee. In the first year Lopez collects an income from the assets amounting to £10,000. He puts it into the John Doe Trust account and there it sits. But back in London, the Inland Revenue writes to Doe saying, in effect, 'You have the power to enjoy Lopez's £10,000 because, say, if you went to Uruguay you could order him to pay it to you. So under these new sections of the Finance Act we are assessing you for income tax this year on your normal British income *plus* that £10,000 in Uruguay.'

Using the Act, the Inland Revenue slapped assessments on William's executors and on Edmund for four tax years, 1937–41. They assessed William's executors for surtax on £1.06 million and Edmund for surtax on £1.17 million. When the Vesteys resisted, they were compelled to disclose all sorts of documents – bank accounts, balance sheets, schedules of investments, and schedules of liabilities and assets. But when it came to the original accounts and books of the Paris trust, the Inland Revenue was thwarted. As the Commissioners of the Inland Revenue reported, '[These] were not before us. They were last known to be in a box at Bordeaux, where they had been left in June, 1940, at the time of the German occupation of France, and their present whereabouts was not known.'

The Revenue prepared its case with care. Before the Commissioners on December 21–22, 1942, it argued that most of the £960,000 annual rent from Union to the Paris trustees had made its way back to Western United Investment company. Sometimes the trustees paid the money into their own banking account in Amsterdam, but when the war started they paid the money direct to Western. This money, the Revenue said, was then employed by Western for the benefit of William and Edmund in the form of interest free loans. Overall the Revenue argued that the 1921 lease and deed were contemporaneous instruments, the product of a scheme to avoid United Kingdom taxation. William and Edmund had the power to enjoy the trustees' income because they had the power to direct the investment of the income in loans to themselves.

The Special Commissioners agreed with the Revenue. New information about the Vesteys' finances had emerged during the hearing and the assessments on the two brothers were increased. William's executors were now assessed to £1.8 million and Edmund to £2.1 million. The Vesteys appealed to the High Court. The case took nearly four years to get there and in the meantime the Revenue, which had continued to investigate the Paris trust, came up with further assesments. By 1944 William's executors had been assessed to £2.15 million and Edmund to £2.37 million, and before the legal battle was finally over, the Vesteys faced the possibility of having to pay £10 million in back tax and surtax (£88 million at today's values).

The case came before Mr Justice Macnaghten in the King's Bench division in October 1946 and lasted seven days. There was a glittering array of legal talent in court because, as the judge noted, 'the amount at stake in these appeals is immense'. Sir Patrick Hastings, KC, appeared for the Vesteys and Sir Frank Soskice, KC, for the Crown. Both were regarded as leading silks of their day. It was clear from the interest the case created that both sides considered that more was at stake than the money; for the Vesteys, the future of their Paris trust; for the Revenue, the effectiveness of the new sections of the Finance Act.

The Vesteys first attempted a quick kill. All the facts in this case, they pleaded, had already been disclosed in the 1931 case (see Chapter 3) and were, therefore, well-known to the Inland Revenue authorities long before the present assessments were made. The law said that the income tax inspector could only make new assessments if he discovered some relevant fact previously unknown to him. In this case, the Vesteys said, the inspector had not discovered any new fact, only a new point of law, and the assessments were therefore invalid. Macnaghten rejected this argument, and the case came down to the direct question: did the Vesteys have the power to enjoy the income of the Paris trustees?

Macnaghten was in no doubt. 'To say that a person enjoys an income of so much a year is a common expression: its meaning is, I think, well understood. It means in common parlance that the income belongs to that person, and that he is free . . . to spend it or save it, or give it away as he pleases because it belongs to him. The income of £960,000 a year, though payable to the Paris trustees, did not belong to them; it belonged to Lord Vestey and his brother, and each could compel the Paris trustees to pay one half of that sum to him. They, therefore, had the power to enjoy the income of the Paris trustees.'

The Vesteys and the Crown both appealed. (Macnaghten had found against the Crown on two of the minor assessments.) The case came before Lords Justices Tucker, Somervell and Evershed in July 1947 and lasted seven days. Again Sir Patrick Hastings appeared for the Vesteys and Sir Frank Soskice for the Crown. On July 30 judgment was given against the Vesteys in all three cases. All three judges were in no doubt that the Vestey brothers had the power to enjoy the income of the Paris trustees. 'It was submitted on behalf of the Crown that . . . the Vesteys could direct that in any given year the rent and the settled fund or any part of it should be lent to either of them without security and at no interest or at a purely nominal rate of interest,' Lord Justice Somervell said. 'I think this is right, I think that they could do this, and they could also direct that there should be loans in the same way to any company in which they were interested, and, as the lease shows, there were a number of companies in which they held all the shares . . . '

In fact, Lord Justice Somervell found, the Vesteys had the power to direct the trust as they wished. 'They have the right of removing and appointing trustees. On the evidence I think the inference is clear. In a scheme of this sort, those concerned work together. The Vesteys were entitled to get, and no doubt did get, trustees who fell in with their views. Was the benefit received by virtue of these rights? Unless the Vesteys had the rights which they had, and perfectly legitimately had under the scheme, it seems impossible to believe that the funds would have been dealt with as they were, i.e. deposited with a company which was allowing overdrafts of a million or so to continue without earning any interest.'

As for the purpose of the whole arrangement, Lord Justice Somervell noted, 'There is no dispute here that there was a transfer of assets within the meaning of the section, and there was a finding, which was not disputed before us, that the main purpose of the creation of the rent and its transfer to the settlement trustees was the avoidance of United Kingdom taxation which would normally accrue on their [the Vesteys] becoming resident.' But the new legislation in 1936 and 1938 had brought the

Vesteys into the tax net, and 'the result is that, in my view, the whole of the income of the trustees has to be deemed to be the income of the Vesteys.'

The other judges agreed. Lord Justice Evershed said, 'I think that it was fundamental to the whole arrangement that the sums of rent as they came to the hands of the Paris trustees and the "capitalised sum" representing the previous instalments of rent, should remain at the disposal of the two brothers Vestey for whatever purposes of their own they respectively required them.' And Lord Justice Tucker said, 'There is really only one conclusion that can be drawn . . . namely that the advances made by the Paris trustees to the Western United Investment Company, coupled with the loans by that company to Lord Vestey and Sir Edmund Vestey, amounted to the receipt of benefit by the Vesteys.'

It has been necessary to go into the details of these judgments in the High Court and the Court of Appeal in order to highlight what happened next. The Vesteys appealed to the House of Lords and there won on every point. The lay reader will find the Law Lords' judgment bewildering, contrary to commonsense, and infuriating in its pedantic approach. In all the earlier hearings the judiciary appears to have based its approach by looking at the Vesteys' arrangements as a whole, deciding whether the purpose was to avoid tax, and if so whether the Inland Revenue assessments were justified.

The attitude of the Law Lords was different. They did not doubt for a moment that the Vesteys' scheme was to avoid tax. As Lord Morton said, 'In our view it was the Vesteys' personal desire to reside in this country which led to the lease of the deed, and the main purpose of the creation of the rent and its transfer to the trust was the avoidance of United Kingdom taxation.' The question to which the Law Lords addressed themselves was whether Parliament had in fact closed the loophole which had allowed the Vesteys to get away with their tax dodge: 'The question is whether the Finance Act of 1936, or alternatively, of 1938, was so framed as to make the Vesteys liable.' And the Law Lords set about answering this question, supplying to the words used in the Acts and in the trust deed 'the ordinary principles of construction, without regard to the fact that the trust deed is part of a scheme of tax avoidance'.

Once the Law Lords had adopted this principle they were no longer looking at the tax-dodging activities of the Vesteys but at the skills of legal draftsmanship of the Treasury lawyers who had worked on the 1936 and 1938 Finance Acts, and the whole emphasis of the case had changed. Their Lordships were not impressed; and as they proceeded to tear apart the wording of sections under which the Inland Revenue had made its assessments, the Treasury lawyers must have been squirming in their Whitehall offices.

The other judges had found that the Vesteys had had the *power* to enjoy the income of the Paris trustees. The Law Lords asked, what is meant by the word power? Subsection 3 of the Act says, 'An *individual* shall be deemed to have the power if the *individual* is able in any manner whatsoever to control the application of the income.' And on this definition, with the word *individual*, the whole Inland Revenue case against the Vesteys began to come unstuck. For the Law Lords found that neither William nor Edmund Vestey had any *individual* right to control the application of the trustees' income: they had only a *joint* right, neither could act alone, *both* their signatures were required, or orders had to come from *both* brothers before the Paris trustees would obey. As Lord Simonds put it, 'Lord Vestey as an individual acquired no individual right. The Interpretation Act cannot be invoked to convert singular into plural. Just as it is the income of an individual that is being assessed, so it is the right of that individual that must be regarded. Whatever view is taken, then, of the right to direct investment, that was not a right of Lord Vestey alone, and it cannot be said that by virtue of that right he is brought within the section of the Finance Act.'

Worse was to come. Even if the Crown had proved to some judges' satisfaction that the Vestey brothers had enjoyed interest-free loans which had originated from the Paris trust income, this still did not bring them into the tax net. Lord Simonds said, 'It appears to me that, apart from all other difficulties, to say of a man who may direct that the trust income should be invested in a loan to himself that he has the beneficial enjoyment of that income is a misuse of language . . . Lord Vestey is liable if it can be said of him that he is able in any manner whatsoever, and whether directly or indirectly, to control the application of the income. But leaving aside the fact that Lord Vestey by himself can do nothing, a right to direct investment is not a control of the application of the income. The latter words point to an out-and-out disposal of the income for the benefit of some person or persons and are wholly inappropriate to an investment by way of loan.'

Lord Normand put the finishing touches to the demolition of the Inland Revenue's case. 'Parliament in its attempts to keep pace with the ingenuity devoted to tax avoidance may fall short of its purpose,' he said. 'That is a misfortune for taxpayers who do not try to avoid their share of the burden, and it is disappointing to the Inland

Revenue, but the Court will not stretch the terms of the taxing Acts in order to improve on the efforts of Parliament and to stop the gaps which are left open by the statute. Tax avoidance is an evil, but it would be the beginning of much greater evils if the Courts were to overstretch the language of the statute in order to subject to taxation people of whom they disapproved.'

There are indications that throughout this long and costly case the Vesteys remained confident that they would win in the end. One indication is that when the case was still before the Commissioners of Inland Revenue the Vesteys were offered an adjournment to enable them to collect further evidence so as to convince the Commissioners that they had not received loans or advances from the Paris trust. The Vesteys refused the offer, saying that they would stand or fall on the wording of the Finance Acts of 1936 and 1938, a decision that proved absolutely correct. The other indication is that even as the Inland Revenue challenged the Vesteys' tax arrangements and started the legal action that was to last for seven years, the Vesteys were repeating the 1921 manoeuvres that had enabled them to protect their wealth from the Inland Revenue.

William had seen the 1921 settlement serve out his lifetime. But Edmund was still hearty and there was a new generation to protect – William's heir, Samuel, the new baron; and Edmund's son, Ronald. In 1942 the first settlement had run its course and the Vesteys had to decide what to do about it. They could have renewed it on virtually the same terms. Instead they decided to move even further offshore. From a purely business point of view this made sound sense. Singapore had just fallen, the Germans were at the gates of Moscow, and the Americans had barely recovered from Pearl Harbor. Many of the

Vestey assets were in neutral countries. If the ownership of these assets was also in neutral hands then the Vestey empire would be protected from German seizure if Hitler invaded Britain.

So the Vesteys appointed as trustees of the 1942 settlement James Flynn, an employee of the Vesteys, but a resident of Uruguay, a neutral country, and Reginald Stephens Beak, another employee of the Vesteys, but a resident of Argentina, another neutral country. Flynn and Beak must have been highly trusted employees because the Vesteys gave them the bulk of their international operation. This was the essential difference between the 1921 settlement and the 1942 settlement. In 1921 the Vesteys only handed to the trustees *control* of their assets abroad; in 1942 they transferred to the trustees *ownership* of those assets. From this moment on, the Vestey empire outside the United Kingdom was owned by people who were not resident in Britain, and the trustees appointed over the years have all resided outside the United Kingdom. Over the years they have been: Mark Stephen Drabble, appointed September 17, 1959; Henri Marion, appointed June 13, 1967; Claude Thurel, appointed December 6, 1967; Peter Alan Beak, appointed November 27, 1970, and Ronald Charles Grove,* appointed January 20, 1971.

The list of assets handed to the trustees makes impressive reading. They included:

Freezing works or cold storage premises: Brazil 4, Argentina 1, USA 2, Germany 1, Spain 2, Portugal 1.

Land and buildings in China.

* Grove was kidnapped by Argentine guerrillas in 1972. The Vesteys asked the British Foreign Office and the Buenos Aires police to keep out and negotiated and paid an undisclosed ransom. Rumour in Argentina was that it was $1 million. Grove was released unharmed.

Land, a warehouse, and an office in Portugal.
A cork factory in Spain.
Meat Depots: Brazil 1, Argentina 3.
Land and properties in Brazil registered in the name of the Lancashire General Investment Company: ten properties and titles.
Land and property in Colombia.
Land in Paraguay.
Freezing works, packing plants, warehouses, buildings, structures etc: China 6, Venezuela 1.
Other investments in Venezuela: cattle ranches 8, fattening paddocks 3, stockyards and paddocks 8, houses and offices 3.

As well, the trustees of the 1942 settlement came to own, directly or through nominees, all the shares in three offshore companies: the Commercial Insurance Corporation, of Jersey; the Commercial Investment Company of Bermuda, and the Salient Shipping Company (Bermuda) Ltd. The first two companies are general holding and investment companies. The Salient Shipping Company also has general investments but is mainly a ship owner and chartering company. Its ships are almost all chartered to the Blue Star Line. All three companies are highly profitable, so the original asset value of the empire handed to the trustees in 1942 – valued at £18 million in 1921 – is today worth many times that sum.

Once the trustees were in possession of these Vestey assets, they immediately leased them again to Union, as in 1921, for the same annual rental of £960,000. (This was renewed in 1963 and again in 1984.) The structure of the trust was also changed in 1942. The £960,000 which Union paid to the trustees was placed in a rental fund into which also flowed the dividends from the three offshore companies. The trustees invest the money in the rental fund to produce what the trust deed calls 'the annual income', which the trustees then divide in two, paying one half into 'Edmund's Fund' and the other half into 'Samuel's Fund'. In 1966, the only year for which figures have ever been revealed, Edmund's Fund had assets of £4,197,000 (£15 million at today's values) and Samuel's Fund had £5,105,000 (£18 million). In that year alone the income of each fund was about £300,000 (£1 million). These assets represented merely the accumulation of income, not the original capital, and the income mentioned is 'income from invested income', harking back to William's early principles.

The 1942 trust provided that the money in each fund was to be allowed to accumulate until, when directed by the manager of each fund, the trustees were to make occasional and discretionary payments to the beneficiaries. These managers were clearly people of power, so over the years they have been various Vesteys. Samuel's Fund was managed by his son, William, until William was killed in action in Italy in June 1944, while serving as a captain in the Scots Guards. Edward Brown, the family's trusted financial adviser, then took over until 1966. Since then the present Lord Vestey has managed the fund for his branch of the family. Edmund's Fund, representing the other branch of the family, was managed by Edmund's son, Ronald, from 1942 to 1987.

The trust was still the Paris trust in the sense that it was in Paris that the trustees usually met, but only at infrequent intervals. But, unlike the 1921 trust, the 1942 one was written under the laws of Northern Ireland. The reason is an intriguing one. English law has always been concerned that property should not be tied up for excessively long periods; hence the medieval statute of *mortmain* preventing this. The present law for England is embodied in the Perpetuities and Acccumulations Act 1964. This allows the Vesteys to leave the assets, or income from them, with the trustees until whichever date is the earlier of the following three events: twenty years after the death of the last survivor of the children of the person who set up the trust; or, twenty years after the death of all the children, living at the date of the settlement, of King Edward VII; or January 1, 2030.

However English law no longer allows the income of a trust to be *accumulated* for more than twenty-one years, no matter what the length of the trust itself. The reason for this is that in 1796, a London merchant, an immigrant from Geneva called Peter Thellusson, died leaving what was in those times a massive fortune of over £600,000. In his will he directed that this be invested and allowed to accumulate during the maximum life of a trust, so that the ultimate fund would be divided into three parts for the anticipated eldest son of the eldest son of each of his three sons.

When the will was published the authorities did some hurried calculations which showed that the eventual accumulation of the re-invested income of £600,000 could, by the date of the pay out, be greater than Britain's National Debt. The government could do nothing to alter Thellusson's trust, but rapidly passed a law to prevent such a thing happening again – the Accumulations Act 1800, which is still in force. (In the event, Thellusson's sons went to law to try to set aside their father's trust. They failed but the cost of litigation over several years so depleted the £600,000 that the eventual accumulation turned out to be modest compared with the National Debt.)

But, the Accumulations Act does not apply to Northern

Ireland, and by writing the 1942 trust under the laws of Northern Ireland the Vesteys avoided limiting the period over which they could allow the income of the trust to accumulate. So it would appear that another element of the Vestey family's grand design was that an income, planned to be free of tax, would be invested and only from the proceeds of that second investment would the family draw for its needs. The bulk, following William's original frugal example – 'I live on what I earned twenty years ago' – would be accumulated for the longest possible period. (We will discuss later the magnitude of the sums this could produce.)

The Vestey family appears to have considered – certainly at the time of the 1942 trust and probably before – how it could best avoid the internal dissent that such a trust produced in the Thellusson family, and how it could maintain the tight, centralised, and devoted control that had made the business prosper. It is clear that William and Edmund decided very early on that it would not be a good idea to bring all their sons into the business and that to prevent envy and jealousy, those who did not join in controlling the family empire should be adequately compensated. So, for example, in 1928 William provided his second son George Ellis Vestey with a large house on one of the finest sporting estates in the north of England, Warter Priory. But *ad hoc* compensation such as this did not appeal to the brothers' orderly minds, so in 1935 they worked out a way of looking after other members of the family.

The main trust with the mainstream of the Vestey assets would be for the chosen representatives of the two branches of the family (not necessarily the eldest son; Edmund chose Ronald, his youngest son, to represent his branch). The other members of the family would be provided for by other trusts set up with cash or assets no longer directly necessary to the operation of the business. William and Edmund set up the first of these smaller trusts in 1935 with assets – buildings and warehouses in China – for Edmund's family, which by the time of the 1942 main trust consisted of eight adults and six infant beneficiaries. The assets of this trust were increased on March 30, 1942 – five days after the main trust had been re-created – when Ronald Vestey covenanted to pay into it £2.3 million.

Why did he do this? This lesser trust is of the same Byzantine complexity as the main one, with three successive bodies of trustees, and its operations are just as secret. But it seems likely that this payment by Ronald Vestey represented some form of equalisation or compensation – since the main trust was already of far greater value – to Ronald's brothers, sisters, nephews and nieces who were not beneficiaries of the main trust. A court case in 1950, *Lloyds Bank v O'Meara*, revealed a little of the size of this lesser trust. It had at that time assets of about £4.6 million (about £34 million at today's values) producing an income of about £126,000 a year.

The wisdom of all this is apparent. Although the family has multiplied over the years there have been no public disputes over succession to the Vestey empire and no disaffected Vestey has revealed any family secrets. To the outside world the Vesteys have remained as united and as discreet as William and Edmund could ever have wished them to be.

8

The New Generation

A postwar fight for markets

The Vesteys welcomed the end of the war with great relief. They had had a bad time. William had died in 1940, Evelyn five months later, so they had not seen their much-cherished Blue Star shipping line virtually wiped out by German U-boats. The sinkings that had so distressed Evelyn in 1940 continued to the end of 1944. Blue Star began the war with thirty-eight ships and later added a further three. It lost twenty-nine to enemy action, some with all hands; the twelve ships that survived made the company a shadow of its earlier self. Yet at the very time that the family needed young and vigorous leadership to re-establish its empire it also lost its heir apparent, William Howarth Vestey, only son of the second Baron, Samuel. William Howarth, a captain in the Scots Guards, was killed in action in Italy in June, 1944.

Edmund and William's father, Samuel, had to carry on, tackling with Ronald Vestey's help a world much changed by the war. In Britain the family faced the threat of nationalisation; abroad the cheap and docile labour that had made their South American operation so profitable had gone. Strikes, new wage demands, a changed attitude of governments, threats of revolution, and the possible loss of their traditional Chinese operation to the Americans, kept the family occupied in the early days of peace.

The Labour Party policy in the postwar period was to nationalise cold storage and the importation and wholesale distribution of meat. In the event this never came about, but the Vesteys took precautions nevertheless. At an extraordinary general meeting of Union Cold Storage in July, 1949, Samuel, the second Baron, explained what these were and why he considered them necessary. 'We feel that these proposals for nationalistation are only a step on the way to the general nationalisation of all business in this country,' he said. 'This could only mean the ruin of our country and finally the establishment of a slave state. We feel that the time has come when this should be plainly stated . . . and it is up to everyone to do all he possibly can to prevent it.' The Vesteys' proposals were to change the name of the company to Union International Limited and then to transfer the assets of the cold storage side of the new company's operations to the old Union Cold Storage Company Limited. 'This will protect the other parts of the business in the unfortunate event of these proposals of the Labour Party eventually being carried out.'

The family's problems in Britain turned out to be easy to handle compared with their difficulties overseas. First there was China, one of the countries which had contributed largely to the making of their original fortune. The Chinese egg trade had grown so much that by 1939 the value of eggs which the Vesteys and other British concerns were importing from China had reached £3 million a year. But as early as April, 1945, with the war still raging in the Pacific, the Vesteys learnt that American companies were planning to move into this market the moment that the war ended and had already placed orders for the manufacture of egg drying equipment. The Vesteys moved swiftly. They applied to the Foreign Office for permission and travel documents to send three egg experts to Chungking to negotiate a deal with Chiang Kai-Shek's government, and to erect as soon as possible a dried egg plant. Their application got caught up in Whitehall war-time bureaucracy: the Foreign Office said it was not their concern but that of the Department of Overseas Trade. The DOT said that its policy was to limit activities in China to investigations and making contacts, and to avoid actual commitments. In the long run, this delay did not matter. The Communist take-over ended the egg trade and although the Vesteys hung on in China until the early fifties the doors eventually closed on them, probably for ever.

In Argentina, Juan Perón had taken over the Department of Labour in 1943. Perón, by stimulating labour organisations, especially in the overseas-owned packing plants, and promoting the interests of the workers, made the department into a political base which eventually helped to carry him into the presidency. The Vesteys, unusually for them, did not fully appreciate the changes taking place in Argentina and failed to react in time. They refused to recognise or negotiate with the meatworkers' unions and adopted such an unyielding attitude to their workers' demands that the Foreign Office in London became worried that they were encouraging anti-British feeling. Memos flew. 'Vesteys in Argentina are considered to drive a very hard bargain generally,' wrote one Foreign Office official. 'And they do not enjoy a particularly high reputation. It is not surprising, therefore, that they should be picked upon by professional agitators.'

The British ambassador in Buenos Aires, Sir David Kelly, thought much the same. 'Neither the British nor American *frigoríficos* show as much sympathy as they might in the handling of their workers. Vesteys, as you know, have a reputation for being ruthless employers and discipline may be rather strict.' (To this an official in the South American Department of the Foreign Office added the handwritten cryptic comment, 'At one time, nevertheless, they were said to adopt Nelsonian tactics with regard to the behaviour of their senior personnel in Buenos Aires.' The main problem was the quality of the Vestey management. The general manager in the late 1930s was Reginald Beak, who had married Betty, the daughter of the founder of the Las Palmas plant at Zarate, the foothold of the Vesteys in Argentina. His management staff consisted largely of young English barristers sent out from London who could hardly speak Spanish. Beak maintained a British Empire mentality and at a crucial time in Argentine political development failed to understand what was going on. When Perón organised his first protest march against foreign investors, hordes of screaming men marched up Diagonal Norte with banners calling for death to the foreigners and for the confiscation and nationalisation of their assets. Beak and an assistant watched them from the balcony of the Vestey offices. Beak, unprepared for this, was aghast and frightened. 'My God,' he said. 'What's going to happen to us?' His assistant replied, 'You brought it on yourselves.'

The Vesteys' relations with the Argentine workers came to a head late in 1945. The Vesteys refused to co-operate with a newly-created labour relations board that was supposed to establish minimum wages. The packing house unions responded by calling a general strike. After three months of violence, the government, under Perón's urging, declared the strike to be legitimate, decreed that working hours in the packing plant's freezing rooms should be reduced and publicly condemned the Vesteys and other foreign-owned packing plants for their refusal to compromise. In March 1946, the Vesteys surrendered. They promised to comply with a minimum wage decree, they agreed to co-operate with the labour commission, to provide job stability, and to offer a full day's pay for six hours' work in the freezing rooms. From that moment, the Vesteys realised that their days in Argentina were probably numbered. Perón came to power the following year and made it clear that he was determined to end Argentina's semi-colonial economy. Meat exports to Britain slumped and even though there was some improvement when Perón's regime ended in 1955 they never again rose to their earlier levels.

The Vesteys had accepted this state of affairs and were already winding down their Argentine operation when the Argentine government initiated a monopoly trial against the Vesteys, the American company Swift, and a large locally-owned packing house, Fasa, in 1970. Swift and Fasa both declared themselves bankrupt but the Vesteys' earlier preparations enabled them to close their packing plant down in an orderly manner and pay off all their employees. The family still kept a small soap factory, a chicken farm, and a shipping and forwarding agency in Argentina but its long history there effectively ended in

May, 1971 when the Anglo packing house at South Dock processed its last ton of meat under Vestey ownership.

No doubt the Vesteys would have got out of Argentina more quickly if prospects elsewhere in South America had been brighter. Their business in Brazil continued to prosper but in Venezuela where they owned large tracts of land they feuded with the government, with the British consul, British ambassador, a visiting British MP, and the British Foreign Office. The trouble began when the Vesteys sent two young trainees to Venezuela to work on Vestey ranches. In Caracas, the trainees found that the terms of their contract – they were expected to buy their own saddles, and part of their salary was to be withheld against any unexpected, unforeseen circumstances – were so severe that they would have barely sufficient money left on which to live. So they went to the British Consul and asked him if he thought that the arrangement was a fair one. When he said he did not, the trainees refused to take up their jobs and eventually the Vesteys had to pay their fares back to Britain. The Vesteys, infuriated, accused the consul of unjustified interference and complained to the Foreign Office.

The British embassy in Caracas defended the consul vigorously. 'I should have thought that it was a consul's duty to interfere to prevent British subjects being exploited, even by other British subjects,' the First Secretary wrote. 'I am afraid I do not attach much importance to [the Vesteys'] statement that two earlier trainees, engaged on the same terms, are perfectly satisfied. They were taken to the interior immediately on landing. They had no opportunity of learning about local conditions and are to all intents and purposes incommunicado.' The incident, not important in itself, did, however, bring to the fore a long-standing wish by the British ambassador in Caracas, Sir George Ogilvie Forbes, to take up with the Foreign Office the Vesteys' general attitude in Venezuela. He got off a quick cable:

'Chairman of Venezuelan Development Commission having enquired of me why [Vestey] have sent their worst men to Venezuela I replied half-jokingly that I would look into the matter on condition that Venezuelan government removed cattle transition tax which makes business impossible. To my surprise he informed me yesterday that necessary amending legislation would soon be passed. Must now try to persuade the present management whose name stinks here and whose derelict plant is an eye-sore to British prestige to set their house in order in a manner more acceptable to Venezuelan government.'

Sir George's hand was reinforced by the visit to Venezuela of a British MP, Wing Commander Hulbert. Hulbert asked a Venezuelan official to arrange a meeting with the Vestey local manager. But the manager sent the official packing, calling him 'a spy of the government'. Hulbert, not impressed with what he had seen and heard, wrote a two-and-a-half-page report for the Foreign Office on his return to London in which he said that the Vesteys' position and plant in Venezuela were 'a disgrace to British industry' and announced his intention of calling on the Vesteys to tell them so and to ask Ronald Vestey to make an early visit to Venezuela and do something about it.

Pending this approach, Sir George wrote a long letter to the Foreign Office setting out in detail what he thought of the Vestey operation in Venezuela. 'Vesteys seem to take an apathetic and even bloody-minded view of Venezuela and with their large estates have been mere passengers in the boat and have contributed, in proportion to their resources, little or nothing to increase the food supply of this country in these times of grave crisis . . . Moreover they have treated their staff abominably and have only themselves to thank for the resultant embezzlements and other misdeeds . . . The Venezuelan government's main complaint against the management can be best summed up in the phrase "attitude of mind". The company apparently does not yet realise that the days of regarding Latin Americans as "Dagos" are long past.'

The combined weight of the Foreign Office, one of its ambassadors, and a leading British MP got nowhere. The concluding note on the Foreign Office file says despondently: 'Wing Commander Hulbert came to see me today. He said that he had failed utterly to put any good advice across to Vesteys and had been given to understand that they did not need advice from anyone on how to run their business. Nor did Ronald Vestey have any intention of going out to Venezuela.'

Longevity runs in the Vestey family. William lived to eighty-one. His son Samuel stood in the wings, ready to take over the Vestey empire, for nearly fifty years, but first William, and then Edmund blocked his way. In the early fifties, Edmund, eighty-four, remained in control as chairman of Union International, allowing Samuel to stand in for him only when he was ill. The situation intrigued the City reporters for the national newspapers, and gossip columnists followed their lead. This led to some embarrassment for the Vesteys. On January 5, 1951 the *Evening Standard* diary went into some detail about the family trust and followed this with some personal details about Lord Samuel Vestey.

'He is tallish, clean-shaven and white-haired. He has a

trick of screwing up his eyes and gazing appraisingly at his companions through rimless eyeglasses. He goes to the company headquarters in Smithfield every day from his town house in Manchester Square. He works from ten until six in his plainly-furnished office. Lord Vestey used to hunt with the Cotswold. His sport now is shooting. Since boyhood Lord Vestey has collected stamps. He has a first rate collection and keeps the most valuable in a safe deposit. His Gloucestershire house, Stowell Park, is picturesque with gables and battlements. He is believed to be one of the first to benefit from the million-a-year trust set up by his father, William, and uncle, Edmund.'

Unfortunately, the very same day as the *Evening Standard* report appeared, the *Daily Telegraph* carried an amazing news item about Edmund Vestey. A solicitor had appeared before the East Kent Valuation Panel the previous day to appeal for Sir Edmund's rates to be reduced on the grounds that he could not afford to pay them! He asked for a reduction from £497 rateable to £320 rateable. In a letter read to the court, Sir Edmund said, 'We have reached the point when we have to decide whether we shall be able to reduce our expenses or move out of this house.' The solicitor said that the grounds of Thanet Place required at least five gardeners and the house a minimum staff of six. It might be said that the house was built to suit Sir Edmund, but since that time conditions were for him – and many other people – far from the same. The panel was not impressed and refused the application.

When Sir Edmund died two years later, leaving £173,000, the popular press remembered this case and called him 'the millionaire who claimed to be hard up'. But other obituaries were effusive. *The Times* said that Union

International and the Blue Star Line were 'the monument to the foresight, acumen and industry of the brothers'. It said that the way the Vestey family empire had prospered was among the romances of history. It praised Edmund's patriotism and said his baronetcy in 1921 had been for 'placing at the disposal of the government all the vast resources of the company in cattle and cold storage accommodation'.

Edmund set out in his will how he would like the Vestey dynasty to proceed. 'No amount of money which I could have given my son Ronald in his youth could have compared with the happiness and usefulness he has derived from the occupation and training throughout his business career which I have seen that he has received from the time I took him into my business at the age of seventeen. So, in their turn, my male descendants will be dependent upon him for training and development for their business careers. Just as I have seen to his training, I express to my son Ronald my desire that he will see that my other male descendants secure preferential treatment as regards position in the business. It will be his duty to extend good offices and render other assistance to members of our family according to their merits, abilities and necessities.'

Like William's wife, Evelyn, who had lived for only five months after her husband's death, Edmund's wife, Ellen, died soon afterwards on December 11, 1953. And Edmund's emphasis on the role that his son, Ronald, was to play in the Vestey empire was percipient because Samuel, the second baron, lasted only six months after taking control, dying at his Manchester Square house, aged seventy-one on May 4, 1954. Since his son, William Howarth, had been killed in the war, the title passed to his grandson, Samuel George, who was only thirteen. Working control of the business went to Ronald Vestey.

The probate of the wills of three Vesteys – Edmund, Ellen and Samuel – granted within such a short space of time, attracted attention to the comparatively small amounts of money they left, and John Junor in the *Sunday Express* wrote the first newspaper article critical of the Vestey family and its tax arrangements. It was short, and pungent, and is worth quoting in full.

'So Sir Edmund Vestey, who with his brother, the first Lord Vestey, build a £52 million frozen meat empire and must, in his day, have been one of the richest men in Britain, died worth a mere £175,000 out of which the State collected £95,000 death duties. His fortune, like that of his brother, who left only £261,000, had been whisked beyond reach of the tax collector. Very clever men, these, who manage to live the spacious life of multi-millionaires and die apparently worth only a pittance. There is no illegality, of course, in such transfers of wealth out of the State's clutch. Those who seek the loopholes can find them, though some, like the unlucky Dukes of Devonshire and Bedford, fail to wriggle through in time.

'But what are the consequences to the community? When vast fortunes escape death duties the rest of us have to pay more in taxation to keep the country going. Is that equitable? You know the answer. The tenacity with which some immensely rich men cling to their money is fascinating to those of us who have less to cling to. A member of a very wealthy family told me some time ago that after dinner one of his richer relatives confessed to him that he kept over £2 million in cash in the bank as a standby. He offered my friend an after-dinner cigar, but explained that it would have to be a Jamaican cigar and

William and Edmund, the founders of the Vestey empire, in 1925.

Seated, from left to right: William Vestey, Evelene Brodstone and Edmund Vestey, *c.*1905.

Stowell Park, near Northleach in Gloucestershire, the seventeenth-century manor house bought, with 2,379 acres of land, by Lord Vestey's son Samuel in September 1923.

Sir Edmund Hoyle Vestey with his wife in 1962.

Frank Hardy with aboriginal stockmen in 1973.

Lord and (the first) Lady Vestey at Windsor in July 1977.

Mark Vestey (Lord Vestey's younger brother) next to Prince Charles in the Young England Polo Team in August 1972.

Mark Vestey with his bride Rosie Clifton at their wedding in February 1975.

Michael and Monika Telling on their wedding day in 1981. In 1984 Michael, a cousin of Lord Vestey, was found guilty of the manslaughter of his wife.

Lord and (the second) Lady Vestey at their wedding in 1981.

Lord Vestey in February 1988.

Tim Vestey in 1991.

not a Havana because he couldn't afford Havanas. On the whole I think that there is more fun in being just reasonably comfortable.'

Ronald, the new chief of the Vestey clan, took this in his stride. He had been brought up in the Vestey mould, sent to the outposts of its empire to learn the business and indoctrinated in the family system of running it. He saw unions as opposition and felt that labour had to be watched constantly. There was no part of the vast Vestey enterprise that was too small to merit his attention, no sum of money so little that it could be ignored. It was not that the items or the money were significant in the ultimate profit picture, but that if the edges of the edifice were allowed to crumble then the whole structure could be endangered. A few examples best illustrate the Vestey philosophy.

A passenger on a Blue Star liner swore that when he accidentally broke a water glass his steward, dismayed, said, 'Damn, now we'll have to tell Mr Ronald.' In London the company maintained its own debt collecting department, handling at that time about £100,000 worth of bad debts, mostly from small traders who could not pay for their meat or from tenants who had fallen behind in their rent. It was Vestey policy to sue in the county court for any debt of £1 or over and to evict any tenant who was more than £4 behind in his rent. Two company van drivers who had been caught eating the company's ice cream were sacked immediately and the Vesteys for a while seriously considered trying to instigate criminal proceedings against them.

Ronald would make surprise trips to the outposts of the family empire to keep the employees on their toes. 'You'd get a call from his secretary that he wanted to meet you in the foyer of the Adelphi Hotel, Liverpool at 8 a.m.,' a former employee recalls from his days in the thirties. 'On the stroke of eight Mr Ronald would come out. We'd get into the big Buick – the family owned a hire car firm – and we'd go to the Stanley meat market where we had a stall. Mr Ronald would check the prices and the profit margins. Then we'd drive down to the King's Dock where one of our ships would be in and he'd check the loading. Then he'd go over the ship's store with a torch. Then on to the Lamport and Holt office in the Liver building to see that the manager was on time. He'd leave me on the docks to find my own way back.'

Ronald kept up these spot checks until he was in his eighties. He would leave his house, Thurlow Hall, in Suffolk, at dawn in a chauffeur-driven car and head north. A quick stop at one of the Vestey factories to check on the employees' timekeeping – 'Where's Mr So-and-so [the manager]. Oh, not in yet? What time does he usually come in?' Then on to any High Street for a call at the local Dewhurst butcher's shop. The stories about these calls are legendary. One is that Ronald Vestey would enter the shop incognito, pretend to be a customer, and later report on how he was treated. Another is that when he left the shop he would say to the chauffeur, loud enough for the Dewhurst staff to hear, 'York next,' and actually go to Liverpool. These trips were broken at Ronald Vestey's 100,000-acre estate at Assynt, in Sutherland, where he would spend ten to fourteen days. Then he would drive south down the opposite coast, continuing his spot check calls, until what his staff called 'Mr Ronald's summer tour' ended back at Thurlow Hall.

It was this close attention to the making of money, and the equally close attention to investing it that made Ronald

Vestey a key factor in the family's next confrontation with the Inland Revenue. For Ronald faced the difficulty that many rich men must face: if you are already so wealthy that you have everything you need in life and then you receive even more money, what do you do with it?

9

The Big Pay Out

Ronald's investment reveals all

On July 1, 1967, A. H. Gales, an officer in the surtax section, Inland Revenue, Thames Ditton, Surrey, was struck by something odd while looking through the income tax return of Ronald Arthur Vestey, Great Thurlow Hall, Suffolk. The return, prepared by Edward Brown Junior, son of the man who had set up the Vesteys' tax scheme back in 1921, was for the tax year 1965–66. What caught Gales's eye was the fact that income from interest for that period showed a huge increase over the previous year.

A quick flick through the return showed the officer that this increase seemed to be due to very large investments in local authority loans. Gales was not too concerned about the income tax due on this interest: it had already been deducted at source by the various local authorities. What intrigued the officer was the answer to this key question: where had Ronald Vestey got the money to invest in the loans in the first place? Gales sent off what is known in the

Revenue as a 'fishing letter' addressed to Brown at West Smithfield. The letter was brief, but the questions it posed went right to the heart of the matter.

'With reference to your client's returns of income for the two years ended 5th April, 1966, I observe that his income from taxed dividends, interest, etc. for the year 1965–66 shows a considerable increase compared with the income received by him from those sources for the year 1964–65, due mainly, it seems, to funds on loan to local authorities. Will you please be good enough to let me have details of the funds so invested together with dates of deposits and withdrawals where appropriate. Will you also please state whether the funds in question were previously invested and, if so, how the income therefrom is reflected in your client's returns of income for previous years.'

Brown replied promptly. He set out details of Ronald Vestey's investments with dates of deposits and withdrawals. They made an intriguing picture. On December 2, 1964 Ronald Vestey had deposited £50,000 with Deptford Corporation. He had left it there only eight days before taking it out again and depositing it with the Stroud Rural District Council where he left it until July 21, 1965 before moving it to the Borough of Helensburgh. On the same day as he started this chain of transactions – December 2, 1964 – he also started another chain with £100,000. He deposited this with Paisley Corporation, withdrew it on April 23 the following year and transferred it to East Kesteven Rural District Council. Whatever Ronald Vestey's motives for these transactions – it can hardly have been to chase higher interest rates – Gales drew one immediate conclusion: Ronald Vestey on or about December 2, 1964 found himself with £150,000 to invest. Where had this come from?

The next sentence in Edward Brown's letter provided the answer. 'The funds were not previously invested and were received by Mr Vestey on November 18, 1964 as a capital distribution from the Trustees of Settlement dated March 25, 1942.' At Gales's office in Thames Ditton the words 'trustees of settlement' almost jumped from the page. Gales's routine enquiry had revealed the existence of some sort of trust that had paid to one of the beneficiaries £150,000 in cash. What was this trust? Had anyone else received a pay out? Did the Inland Revenue know about it?

The answer to the last question was, of course, yes. The Vesteys' Paris trust had surfaced again, due to Ronald's investments and Gales's probing, and the matter promptly moved out of Gales's hands to those of more senior officers. They mulled over Brown's reply, and took legal advice over a period of nearly eighteen months. Then on December 9, 1968, they struck. P. Beever, an officer in the Controller of Surtax section at Thames Ditton, sent off a long letter to Brown. 'I assume that this is the settlement whereby the late Sir Edmund Hoyle Vestey and the late Rt. Honourable Samuel, Baron Vestey, settled certain lands, buildings and premises in various parts of the world outside Great Britain and Ireland, for the benefit of the Vestey family,' Beever began.

He then set out a list of seven questions, among them who were the trustees, where did they live, and what payments had been made under the settlement to Ronald Vestey or anyone else. He also asked for copies of the settlement accounts including the balance sheets. The letter included the warning, 'It is now under consideration whether the provisions of Section 412, Income Tax Act 1952, apply to Mr Vestey as a beneficiary of the settlement.'

This time Brown was not so quick to answer. It was not until May 30 the following year that he wrote to Beever. He confirmed that they were talking about the same trust, and he listed the trustees: James Flynn, Henri Marion, and Claude Thurel, all of Paris, and Reginald Stephens Beak, of Buenos Aires. He revealed that the lifetime of the trust had been extended to January 1, 1984.

Then Brown went on to list payments made from the trust between 1962 and 1966: the present Lord Vestey, £923,000; Edmund Hoyle Vestey, £920,000; Ronald Vestey, £365,000; the Hon. Mark William Vestey, £200,000; Mrs Jane McLean Baddeley (Ronald's daughter), £100,000; and Mrs Margaret Payne (Ronald's daughter), £100,000. As for the trust accounts and the balance sheets, Brown's retort was short and sharp: 'The accounts of the settlement are kept abroad and no copies are available.' From these figures it can be seen that the two branches of the family would have received roughly similar totals – £1,123,000 for Lord Vestey's branch, the descendants of William; and £1,285,000, for Edmund Hoyle's branch, the descendants of Edmund – if it had not been the decision to pay the ladies of the family, Ronald Vestey's married daughters, each £100,000. This gesture, more a gift than an obligation since both daughters had married well, was to be of crucial importance in court.

After long correspondence and some preliminary skirmishing the Inland Revenue issued Ronald Vestey with an assessment, mainly to prise more information from him. Although overseas trusts are physically beyond their jurisdiction, the Revenue are not without weapons. Under section 745 of the Taxes Act of 1988 they can issue a legally enforceable notice to a British resident taxpayer to produce documents they consider relevant to an assessment.

Under such a notice, Ronald Vestey had to produce all sorts of information about the Vestey trust, including the trustees' accounts which were kept in Uruguay and audited by a certified public accountant there. Inexorably, the whole ramifications of the Vesteys' tax avoidance scheme emerged: the trust's income, its assets, its investments, its banking arrangements, its beneficiaries and potential beneficiaries.

Then the Revenue revised its assessments on Ronald Vestey and made new assessments on other Vesteys. These were altered as what became *Vestey v Inland Revenue* went through various hearings, but as agreed before the commissioners for the special purposes of the Income Tax Acts the figures are astounding. Ronald Vestey was assessed to income tax and surtax for the years 1963–4 to 1966–67 amounting to £888,500. Edmund Vestey was assessed for income tax on £2,019,236 and surtax on £3,370,639. Lord Vestey, because he was not resident in Britain for part of the relevant tax years was assessed for income tax on only £822,146 and surtax on only £1,371,800. On the £100,000 that she received from the Vestey trust in the tax year 1966–67, Mrs Baddeley – or rather her shocked husband – received a demand from the Inland Revenue for tax and surtax totalling £274,121, more than double the amount she had actually been paid.

The assessments were upheld by the special commissioners in 1974, but Ronald Vestey, who was the test action, appealed and the case went to Mr Justice Walton in the High Court. He referred it back to the special commissioners to make findings of fact and conclusions of law. There were further hearings before the special commissioners and then the case that was to make British legal and taxation history began in earnest before Mr

Justice Walton on April 12, 1978. Mr D. C. Potter, QC, a noted writer on tax matters, and Mr James Holroyd Pearce appeared for the Vesteys; the Solicitor-General, Mr Peter Archer, QC, Mr Michael Nolan, QC, Mr Brian Davenport and Mr Peter Gibson for the Crown.

Looking at the case as a layman it is difficult to escape the conclusion that the Vesteys were very lucky. The main issue – had the founders of the Vestey fortune, William and Edmund, discovered a way round the British income tax laws, and were their descendants still using it? – became lost in a welter of legal and constitutional argument over the role and powers of the Inland Revenue. Law students, for whom the case is required reading, will no doubt argue whether the Inland Revenue brought this result upon themselves by overplaying their hand, so it is convenient to begin by describing the Revenue approach.

What the Inland Revenue did was this. It used section 412 of the Income Tax Act of 1952. This was the old section 18 of the Finance Act of 1936 and section 28 of the Finance Act of 1938 consolidated into a new section. As we have seen before, the Inland Revenue failed to bring William and Edmund into the tax net with earlier acts, but the situation now was very different. William and Edmund were dead and were not obtaining any benefit from the trust. But their descendants were. The question was, did section 412 cover these descendants? The section, it will be remembered, begins, 'For the purpose of preventing the avoiding by individuals ordinarily resident in the UK of liability to income tax by means of transfers of assets, by virtue or in consequence whereof either alone or in conjunction with associated operations, income becomes payable to persons resident or domiciled out of the United Kingdom, it is hereby enacted as follows: where such an individual has by means of any such transfer, either alone or in conjunction with associated operations, acquired any rights by virtue of which he has the power to enjoy any income of a person resident out of the United Kingdom . . . that income . . . shall be deemed to be the income of that individual.' Subsection 2 goes on to say that if the UK resident receives or is entitled to receive a capital sum from an overseas trust, then too, the income of the trustee shall be deemed to be the income of the UK resident.

At first sight this appears to cover everything. The Inland Revenue certainly believed that it did. They argued that it caught the individual who made the original transfer of assets and that it even caught *anyone* who later benefited from that transfer, such as relatives or friends. The issue was settled in the famous *Congreve v Inland Revenue* case in the House of Lords in 1948. In that case Mrs Congreve's father had, prior to the 1936 Finance Act, transferred assets to a foreign company. Mrs Congreve had the power to enjoy the income that those assets produced. But, her lawyers argued, *she* had not made the transfer of assets yet *she* was the taxpayer assessed. Parliament had meant the section to apply only to the person who first set up the tax avoiding scheme, not to relatives or other people who benefited although they had had no hand in the matter.

The Law Lords threw out this argument. Lord Simonds said he did not know what better words could have been used in the section if Parliament wanted to cover a transfer of assets by 'A' by means of which 'B' avoided liability to tax. He regarded the language of the section as plain. 'If there has been such a transfer as is mentioned in the introductory words, and if an individual has acquired the rights referred to in this section [power to enjoy the income of the trustees] then the prescribed consequences follow,'

Lord Simonds said. This had also been the view of the Court of Appeal, so the Inland Revenue felt that there was irrefutable legal backing for their view that section 412 caught not only the individual who made the original transfer of assets, but anyone who later benefited.

To return to our example in Chapter 7, where John Doe of Bayswater, London transferred assets abroad and arranged for the income to be paid into the John Doe Trust in Uruguay, with Juan Lopez as trustee. We saw there how Doe was liable for tax as soon as the Inland Revenue could show that he had the power to enjoy the income Lopez received as the result of the transfer of assets. Tax dodgers had got around this by renouncing all rights to the income of the trust and ordering the trustees to accumulate the money for their children when they grew up.

The case of *Congreve v Inland Revenue* confirmed for the Inland Revenue their view that this dodge, too, was ineffective. The moment that the Inland Revenue could show that Doe's children had the power to enjoy the trustees' income, then it could tax them on it, even though the children themselves had nothing to do with the setting up of the original tax avoidance scheme. The Inland Revenue saw an important point of principle here: if they could not tax Doe's children, then tax dodgers could set up overseas trusts for their heirs and a generation later there would be a whole section of the British community enjoying the money in Britain free of income tax.

There was no doubt in the minds of the Inland Revenue officers when they demanded tax from the Vesteys that they were acting correctly under Section 412. The Vestey trust had not been set up by any of those Vesteys whom the Inland Revenue now assessed, but this new generation of Vesteys was liable for tax, the Inland Revenue believed, because each Vestey had *the power to enjoy* the income of the Paris trustees. The Inland Revenue had forced the Vesteys to reveal some of the secrets of the Paris trust, so it knew who had received payments from the trustees, and how much each had received. As far as the Inland Revenue was concerned, there was no better proof that the Vesteys had the power to enjoy the trustees' income than the fact that they had received payment from that income. So it had set about assessing them.

Immediately, interesting options arose. The income which a Vestey had the power to enjoy was not, according to the Inland Revenue's interpretation of section 412, limited in point of time. A Vestey either had the power or he did not. So the Inland Revenue believed that as well as taxing the Vesteys on the trustees' income for that year in which the trustees had in fact paid the Vesteys, they also had the option of taxing them for all the other years, *whether they had received any trust money in those years or not*. In fact, the Inland Revenue claimed that section 412 gave them the power to tax not only *actual* beneficiaries, even in the years when they had received no payment, but also to tax *potential* beneficiaries who at the time of assessment had never received any payments at all.

For the Vesteys, worse was to come. Inland Revenue claimed that section 412 imposed a liability for tax on *each* beneficiary for the *whole* of the trustees' income. Here is an example. In one year the income of the Vestey trust was £600,000. Ronald Vestey got £215,000 but the Inland Revenue believed that it had the right to assess him as if he had received the whole £600,000. Lord Vestey got £123,000 but the Inland Revenue claimed that it could have assessed him, too, as if he had received £600,000. The Revenue said that they were not obliged to collect *all* the tax from one beneficiary. So long as they did not exceed the trust's total income, they could decide which beneficiary to tax and how much he should pay.

The Inland Revenue believed that they were not behaving in an arbitrary fashion; they considered that an important principle was involved, that they were entitled to take into account 'the substantial result and effect of the transaction in question' – in other words, what were the Vesteys up to? The Revenue saw in section 412 a penal element, that, as Lord Greene had put it in an earlier House of Lords tax case, 'A taxpayer who plays with fire has no right to complain if his fingers get burnt.' But were the present generation of Vesteys playing with fire? The Revenue considered that the penal element of section 412 existed not only to punish but to deter. They believed that if a person contemplating an offshore tax avoidance scheme knew that his heirs – the very people for whom 'in consideration of natural love and affection' (as the legal phrase goes) he planned to set up the scheme – would later be taxed so heavily under section 412 as to wish heartily that they had never been made beneficiaries, he would have second thoughts about going ahead.

But applying section 412 in its full strictness appeared so harsh that the Inland Revenue decided to temper their claims – a decision that was to be their undoing. They used their power of 'discretion' which they said that they had in such cases, to assess individuals as they saw fit. They worked out the proportion represented by what a Vestey had received compared with the total income for the trust for each year, and came up with a fifth, a quarter, or whatever. They then assessed that Vestey on that proportion of the trust's income, repeating the procedure for all five tax years, disregarding the fact that in some of those years the Vestey concerned may not have received from the trustees any payment at all.

Again, actual examples will make this easier to understand. Mrs Payne and Mrs Baddeley received nothing until 1966–67 when they each received £100,000. The Inland Revenue took this figure and compared it with the trust's total income year by year, working out the proportion – say one-sixth in 1963–64, one-fifth in 1964–65 and so on – and then assessed the two Vestey ladies for the five-year period. This is why the tax the Inland Revenue demanded from them – £274,121 each – came to more than they had actually received. The Revenue considered that the two women could have been assessed for many times that amount, but by using their discretionary powers and applying the proportion system, they would not be collecting tax on an amount greater than the trustees' income in any one year. This they considered fair and equitable.

The Vesteys, naturally, thought that it was outrageous. Their lawyers argued that no Vestey had any rights which gave him the power to enjoy the trustees' income: a person who was merely a potential beneficiary under a discretionary trust did not have any 'right' in the plain meaning of the word, but only an expectancy. True, a Vestey gained a right when a sum was paid to him, but even then his power of enjoyment could not extend beyond that particular sum, so only that sum could be taxed. For the Vesteys to be liable under section 412, the Inland Revenue would have to prove an objective avoidance of tax: that each of the Vesteys concerned in the case had tried to avoid tax by transferring assets abroad. Clearly none of the Vesteys in this case had done any such thing. Overall, the Vestey lawyers argued that the discretionary power to determine what taxes should be paid and by whom, is vested in Parliament and not with the Inland Revenue. Therefore the Inland Revenue had no right to 'use its discretion' to assess one, or more, of all of the Vesteys in such sums as they thought fit.

This issue of the Inland Revenue's discretionary power appealed to Mr Justice Walton. After a four-day hearing in the Chancery division of the High Court, he delivered judgment on May 26, 1978. An indication of his decision came within one minute of the reading of the judgment. He said, 'So once again the Crown is claiming the right to recover multiple tax from the unfortunate taxpayers, and to recover it year by year quite irrespective of whether the taxpayers do or do not receive anything further out of the settlement funds. If that is what the relevant subsections, on their true construction, do provide, then, of course, so be it . . . There can, however, be no possible burking of the fact that the consequences of the construction which the Crown seeks to place on the relevant subsection produce a monstrous injustice: an injustice so monstrous that the Crown itself in the present case has resiled from its logical consequences and, while claiming a wider right, has sought to attribute to each of the taxpayers only a fraction of the income of the trustees . . . '

The judge dealt speedily with the minor elements of the case. It will be remembered how William's executors and Edmund won their case against the Inland Revenue in 1947. On that occasion for the Crown to show that the two brothers had been brought into the tax net, it had to prove that either of them had 'acquired any right by virtue of which he has . . . power to enjoy' the trustees' income. The Crown had been unable to do that because, as an individual, neither William nor Edmund had any such right;

in order to exercise any right William needed Edmund's permission and Edmund needed William's permission – neither could act alone.

The government thought it had coped with this flaw in the law by an amendment in 1969. The word 'right' vanished from section 412 and the question was solely whether an individual had the power to enjoy the trustees' income. Part of the Inland Revenue claim against the new generation of Vesteys was under the old section and part under the new. The part under the old section failed, Mr Justice Walton found, because once again no Vestey had acquired any right. Here the foresight of Brown senior and the others who had devised the first tax avoidance scheme back in 1921 was readily apparent. The trust was not for a new generation of Vesteys but such was the trust's structure that not one of them had acquired any right to its money. The potential beneficiaries to Edmund's fund or Samuel's fund could not claim any money. They depended on the decision of the manager of each fund, who might or might not decide to give them something. The manager of each fund had himself received payment – Lord Vestey as manager of Samuel's fund, and Ronald Vestey as manager of Edmund's fund. But neither manager had any *right* to receive payment. He could decide to pay himself only with permission from the other manager or the trustees. So the Vestey family had this enormously rich offshore trust in which, legally, no individual Vestey had any right whatsoever.

But what about that part of the Revenue's case under the amended section? That ran into difficulties, the judge said, on another count. The section said power to enjoy *income*. 'Income means income and does not, save as expressly provided, mean or include accumulations of income which have been capitalised,' said Mr Justice Walton. 'It was capital, capitalised income, which was paid out to each of the taxpayers . . . '

It was when he came on to what counsel for the Vesteys had denominated as a serious constitutional question – what rights the Inland Revenue have to pick and choose when recovering tax – that the judge was at his most scathing. He began by taking a simple example: on what basis had the Inland Revenue taken it upon themselves to decide that income tax was not to be charged on a miner's free coal and allowances in lieu thereof? 'I am not arguing the merits or even suggesting some other result . . . should be reached. But this surely ought to be a matter for Parliament, and not the commissioners [of the Inland Revenue]. If this kind of concession can be made, where does it stop; and why are some groups favoured as against others?' Mr Justice Walton asked.

The judge said that, even if contrary to his views, extra-statutory concessions were permissible and did form part of the tax code, they did represent a published code which applied indifferently to all who fell within its scope. 'What is claimed by the Crown now is something radically different. There is no published code and no necessity for the treatment of all those who are *in consimili casu* alike,' the judge said. 'In one case the Crown can remit one third, in another one half, and in yet another case, the whole of the tax properly payable, at its own sweet will and pleasure. If this is indeed so we are back in the days of the Star Chamber.'

Mr Justice Walton then proceeded to take the section to pieces. The relevant income of the trustees could include not only the income they received as a result of the original transfer of assets, but, as the section was worded, the *whole* of the income of the trustees. 'If the settlors in the present case had been unwise enough to select as their foreign resident trustees, say, a New York bank which was trustee of many other settlements as well, the whole of the income of that New York bank . . . the whole of the bank's ordinary trading income, was the income on which the beneficiary . . . could be assessed,' the judge said.

'But the cream of the jest is still to come,' he went on. He quoted one of the provisions of the Vestey settlement which provided for its reconstitution, and cast in the widest possible terms who future beneficiaries might be. The judge said that the terms were so wide that anybody in the United Kingdom, anybody whatsoever, might be included in the reconstituted settlement, and anybody could be assessed for the entire income of the trustees. The judge said that all this was tempered, according to the Crown, by the Inland Revenue's discretion to select who was and who was not to be assessed.

'However, to this submission, counsel for the taxpayers made the acid but fully justified comment that . . . to whomsoever else the Inland Revenue Commissioners were entitled to show discretionary mercy, they were certainly not so entitled to show it to themselves. Nor do I think that they would be entitled to show it to Her Majesty's Ministers of State, who, by their inactivity in this regard, clearly show that they approve of the legislation as it stands. We are therefore doubtless in for an interesting crop of bankruptcies,' the judge said.

'The whole submission, however, is so far removed from reality, from even the most rudimentary notions of justice and fair play, that one had no more than to state it for it to be abundantly obvious that it cannot be maintained. Yet here was the Solicitor-General [Mr Peter Archer, QC] whom we all know as one of the most amiable of men, voluntarily casting himself in the role of Count Dracula. What has gone wrong?

'In my view what has gone wrong is the failure by the courts to correlate the income on which the taxpayer is to be taxed with the income which he has the power to enjoy. I have persuaded myself that what is wrong is the decision of the Court of Appeal in *Lord Howard de Walden v Inland Revenue**. If this decision were to be out of the way and "that income" . . . be taken to be "the income which the taxpayer has the power to enjoy", then the whole section would be quite logical and straightforward. However, standing this decision, I can see no answer to the Solicitor-General's main proposition that if a person receives the income of the settlement to an insubstantial degree, he is nevertheless taxable on the whole income of the trustees. Sitting in this court, I am bound to follow the decision of the Court of Appeal and give effect thereto, monstrous as the result may be.'

So if the Vesteys had based their argument on the lack of logic and justice in taxing the beneficiary on the whole of the trustees' income then they would have lost because the judge considered himself bound by an earlier decision of a higher court. But he was able to find for the Vesteys on two other arguments. First, until any actual payment took place a Vestey was merely a potential beneficiary and had no right to be paid and therefore no right under which he had the power to enjoy the income of the trust fund. And, secondly, income for the purposes of the section

* In 1942 the Court of Appeal upheld the Crown's contention that Lord Howard de Walden who had transferred assets abroad and had subsequently derived a comparatively small benefit from the income from them could be taxed on the *whole* of the income.

did not include accumulations of income which had been capitalised; what had been paid to the Vesteys had been capital and accordingly the question of their having any power to enjoy *income* did not arise. The final result was that assessments on the Vesteys for the amounts they had actually received were left standing; all other assessments and assessments in excess of this were discharged.

This suited neither the Vesteys nor the Inland Revenue. The Vesteys did not see why they should have to pay any tax at all. They wanted their overriding contention tested: that the section applied only to the person who had originally set up the tax avoidance scheme. Mr Justice Walton felt that he was precluded from accepting this because of the House of Lords decision in *Congreve v Inland Revenue*. But the judge's outspoken comments about the Inland Revenue case – 'profoundly disturbing to anyone who cares about equity or equality in taxation, or, more importantly, the rule of law' – encouraged the Vesteys to hope that the House of Lords might consider the highly unusual step of overthrowing one of their own decisions. So they appealed.

The Inland Revenue felt that the whole basis of Section 412, especially its penal element, was being undermined. The Revenue's view had been best expressed by Lord Greene, Master of the Rolls, in the Lord Howard de Walden case: 'The section is a penal one, and its consequences, whatever they may be, are intended to be an effective deterrent which will put a stop to practices which the legislature considers to be against the public interest. For years a battle of manoeuvre has been waged by the legislature and those who are minded to throw the burden of taxation off their own shoulders on to those of their fellow subjects.' So the Inland Revenue appealed. The appeals and cross appeals leapfrogged the Court of Appeal and went direct to the House of Lords. On November 23, 1979 Lord Wilberforce, Viscount Dilhorne, Lord Salmon, Lord Edmund-Davies and Lord Keith of Kinkel began hearing what turned out to be the most important taxation case in thirty-two years.

10

Consternation in the Tax World

The Law Lords explode an atom bomb

The case caused the Law Lords considerable concern. The hearing lasted five days in July, but it was not until November 22, 1979 that they delivered their opinions. As Lord Wilberforce said, the sums involved were large, and important and difficult questions arose for decision. Many people had been taxed on the basis of a previous House of Lords decision, *Congreve v Inland Revenue*, and, said Lord Wilberforce, 'I have reflected with anxiety whether this House ought . . . to depart from it.' Viscount Dilhorne worried abut leaving 'a yawning gap' in the law, and Lord Keith of Kinkel whether 'this is one of those rare cases where it would be proper for this House . . . to depart from one of its own previous decisions'.

Lord Wilberforce went straight to the heart of the case: did the Inland Revenue have a discretion which enabled them to tax one or more or all of the Vesteys in such sums as they thought fit? Before giving his own view, Lord Wilberforce considered some of the practical consequences if this discretion did exist. Firstly, it would be open to the Revenue to select one or more of the Vestey beneficiaries to tax and to pass over the others. Secondly, the Revenue could apportion the tax between several Vesteys according to any method they thought fit – and this without any possibility of appeal because none was provided for. Thirdly, the liability of individual Vesteys would depend on when the Revenue choose to make assessments. For example, by deferring assessments until after 1966–1967 the Revenue had been able to impose liability for 1963–64 upon fresh beneficiaries, Mrs Payne and Mrs Baddeley, who had not received anything until 1966.

'These are some of the consequences, in this case . . . of the Revenue's contention,' Lord Wilberforce said. 'They are frightening enough. But there are more fundamental objections in principle to the whole proposition. Taxes are imposed upon subjects by Parliament. A citizen cannot be taxed unless he is designated in clear terms by a taxing Act as a taxpayer, and the amount of his liability is clearly defined. A proposition that whether a subject is to be taxed or not, or that if he is, the amount of his liability is to be decided by an administrative body, represents a radical departure from constitutional principle. It may be that the Revenue could persuade Parliament to enact such a proposition in such terms that the courts would have to give effect to it. But unless it had done so, the courts, acting on constitutional principles, not only should not, but cannot validate it.'

And that, in brief, was that. Lord Wilberforce had accepted the Vesteys' overriding contention: the Inland Revenue had exceeded their powers. They had no power to use their discretion to decide who should be taxed and how much they should pay. This left the Inland Revenue to reflect that they might have made a tactical error in using their discretion to temper their assessments on the Vesteys and that they might have been better placed before the House of Lords if they had enforced Section 412 to the letter, taxing each and every Vestey on the whole of the trustees' income, however harsh this may have appeared. But this was not the end of the Revenue's humiliation. The Law Lords then moved on to the second question. Had their own House been right in deciding that Section 412 caught not only the man who first set up the tax avoidance scheme but also those who later benefited from it?

The Law Lords looked at the preamble to Section 412 and decided that there were two possible interpretations of it. The first was to regard it as having a limited effect – that it was directed against the actual person who transfers assets abroad, still lives in the United Kingdom, and yet manages to obtain benefits from those assets without paying any tax. The second was to give the whole section an extended meaning so as to embrace all persons, born or unborn, who in any way might benefit from assets transferred abroad by others. The Law Lords were prepared to believe that Parliament intended 'this draconian' tax to be a penal one aimed at deterring tax avoidance schemes, but they could not believe that Parliament meant to penalise 'persons who had no hand in the transfer, who may never benefit from it, who cannot escape it, who remain under liability so long as they live or the settlement lasts.'

Lord Wilberforce said that if the Lords had been correct in the *Congreve v Inland Revenue* case then a result was produced which was arbitrary, unjust, and unconstitutional. 'I find the section, if directed at transferors and benefits taken by them, an ample and powerful anti-avoidance instrument,' he said. 'So I feel not only no need but a great reluctance, in view of the wording used, to extend it against any beneficiary, child, or grandchild, or descendant . . . To penalise is one thing; to visit the sins of the transferor on future generations is quite another.'

The Law Lords were worried about the gap that their decision would leave in the tax laws. Viscount Dilhorne spoke for them all when he said, 'In this complicated case at least one thing is clear and that is the urgent need for reconsideration by Parliament of the terms of Section 412. If the conclusion I have reached as to the construction of the sentence is accepted, then there is indeed a gap to be filled, for then the section only applies to the individual who has sought to avoid tax . . . others who may benefit from the tax avoidance will not be penalised even though they participated in the avoidance. I need not dilate on the injustice which may be suffered by a number of individuals if the *Congreve* construction is applied. They would not I think have grounds for complaint if they were only assessed to tax on the sums they received or were entitled to receive or had power to enjoy. Though a distinction might be drawn between those who participated in the tax avoidance and those who did not. The former category might continue to be assessed to tax on the whole income of the non-resident . . . I hope that in consequence of the light now thrown on Section 412 that section may be speedily amended. In my opinion it certainly should be.'

All five Law Lords dismissed the Inland Revenue appeals and allowed the Vesteys' cross appeals. On the final agreed figures, the Vesteys had been assessed to income tax on £4.37 million and surtax on £7.34 million. As a result of their victory in the Lords they did not have to pay a penny of this tax. This fact did not come across in the first reporting of the case. The Lords had delivered their opinion on a Friday. *The Times* Law Report on Saturday, November 24, headlined 'Arbitrary, unjust and fundamentally unconstitutional', devoted five columns to the case, but the Press in general failed to pick up the issues.

In the taxation world, however, interest was enormous. In the influential *British Tax Review*, Anthony Sumption, a barrister specialising in tax matters, said that the Vestey case had come like an atom bomb to blow *Congreve* away and 'obliterate all the fortifications in defence of the Revenue which had been constructed on the foundation of that case'. Sumption asked what had happened in the thirty-two years since *Congreve* to persuade a House of Lords not noticeably tender to the subject to turn away from that decision 'with expressions of revulsion as strong as any heard in their Lordships' House since the passing of the more robust judges of former times'? He concluded that the Vestey case was an object lesson to judges, including the House of Lords, not to strain the language of statutes or put a gloss on their words. And it was not only the judges who were guilty of this. The Revenue had brought upon themselves the downfall of the section by overplaying their hand. Time and time again they had persuaded the courts to extend their construction of the section until it had finally crashed. 'It is to be hoped that they will rely in future on amending the law rather than persuading courts to strain the words of statutes far beyond the intention of Parliament,' Sumption wrote. 'And if they do follow that course is it too much to hope that much greater skill in drafting the taxing statutes should be employed than has been the case in recent years.'

In the same issue, Milton Grundy, another tax barrister,

said that the Lords' decision had eliminated at one blow all the constitutional and other problems surrounding multiple taxation which the Revenue had previously purported to solve by exercises of administrative discretion. Noting that Viscount Dilhorne had called for reconsideration of the relevant section by Parliament, Grundy said it would be, in his view, a mistake for Parliament to act on the footing that the *Vestey* decision had opened the floodgates to a vast off-shore tax avoidance industry. But until Parliament's intentions were known, tax advisers would be 'in a dark wood, where the way out is hard to see'.

After the *Sunday Times* articles in October, 1980 – 'The Gilded Tax Dodgers' – the Vesteys' tax avoidances schemes and the Lords' decision and the issues it raised – there was widespread public comment. The *Sunday Times* articles had been reinforced with a leading article written by John Whale. 'Here is an immensely wealthy dynasty which for more than sixty years has paid trivial sums in income tax,' Whale wrote. 'All that time its members have enjoyed the considerable pleasures of being rich in England without contributing anything near their fair share to the defences which kept those pleasures in being – against foreign enemies in wartime, against disorder and disease in time of peace. The wealth of the Vesteys, as shopkeepers in this country, has been collected from millions of ordinary people whose tax burdens the family not merely refused to share but actually intensified, since its avoidance increased the sums to be found from non-avoiders . . . There is a view, notably among tax avoiders, that if a thing is not legally actionable it is morally acceptable. But that is to ignore the ill effects of avoidance on less fortunate citizens, and to ascribe to the law a moral reach it cannot possess. The mere fact that they were put to such arcane shifts must have made the Vesteys aware that, within the letter of the law or not, their devices were certainly alien to its spirit.'

In its front page story, the *Sunday Times* also quoted the views of Viscount Simon expressed in an earlier House of Lords tax case, *Latilla v Inland Revenue*: 'Of recent years much ingenuity has been expended in certain quarters in attempting to devise methods of disposition of income by which those who were prepared to adopt them might enjoy the benefits of residence in this country, while receiving the equivalent of such income, without sharing in the appropriate burden of British taxation. Judicial dicta may be cited which point out that, however elaborate and artificial such methods may be, those who adopt them are "entitled" to do so. There is, of course, no doubt that they are within their legal rights, but that is no reason why their efforts, or those of the professional gentlemen who assist them in the matter, should be regarded as a commendable exercise of ingenuity or as a discharge of the duties of good citizenship. On the contrary, one result of such methods, if they succeed, is of course, to increase *pro tanto* the load of tax on the shoulders of the great body of good citizens who do not desire, or do not know how, to adopt these manoeuvres.'

The reaction of its readers surprised the *Sunday Times*. Of the letters it received the following week, three out of four attacked the newspaper for its attitude and supported the Vesteys' actions. 'What a lot of humbug there was in your paper last week (October 5) about the Vesteys, their money and their taxes. As one who is a satisfied customer of Dewhurst the butchers and other Vestey enterprises but far from satisfied with government profligacy, I believe that the money is likely to do me and the country most good if it is left in private hands,' wrote one reader. 'I have read the article in last Sunday's paper with a sense of shock,' said another. 'It is good knock-about Wedgwood-Benn stuff but hardly appropriate to the front page of a responsible newspaper such as yours. It has been laid down by the courts that any taxpayer is entitled so to conduct his affairs as to minimise his liability to tax. So your implication of moral turpitude attaching to the Vestey family is out of place.'

Another reader began, 'Your editorial, "the Morals of the Vesteys" is gutter journalism, ill-informed and demagogic. The top rates of tax on income are not intended to raise revenue in order to pay for defence, law and order, or anything else. They are designed solely to pander to envy. You call the actions of the Vesteys alien to the spirit of the tax law. But the spirit of the British tax law is plunder.' Some readers felt that if there had been any moral wrong-doing it was not on the part of the Vesteys. 'There is no universal moral law to justify taxation at progressive rates,' one reader wrote. 'Indeed to the extent that it is wrong for the majority to use its political power to coerce a minority of individuals into payment of taxes at above average rate, morality points the other way.'

A popular quotation, given as a riposte to the view of Viscount Simon, was that made in 1929 by Lord Clyde: 'No man in this country is under the smallest obligation, moral or other, so to arrange his legal relations to his business or his property as to enable the Inland Revenue to put the largest possible shovel into his stores. The Inland Revenue is not slow – and quite rightly – to take every advantage which is open to it under the taxing statutes for the purpose of depleting the taxpayer's pocket. And the taxpayer is, in like manner, entitled to be astute to prevent, so far as he honestly can, the depletion of his means by the Inland Revenue.' And even among those correspondents who did not support the Vesteys there were some who admitted to other emotions:

'While one cannot condone the behaviour over many years of the Vesteys, one cannot help but admire how successful they have been.'

In *The Times*, the debate was it its fiercest when between professors of law. Two letters set the tone of the exchange. Professor H.W.R. Wade, QC, of Gonville and Caius College, Cambridge wrote, 'It was only by a strained and unnatural construction of a series of Finance Acts that the Vestey beneficiaries could be taxed on income which in fact they had never received. Even if this was right, as the House of Lords held in 1948, the Acts gave (in Lord Wilberforce's words) "no guidance or indication whatever as to what is to be done if there is more than one individual to whom either sub-section may apply." So each one of a group of beneficiaries had to be held liable to tax on the whole of the income of the trust and not merely on his own share of it. A more unjust and clumsy law it would be difficult to imagine.

'But instead of taking steps to correct it, the authorities preferred to preserve it in this indefensible form and to temper its injustice by demanding from each beneficiary only what they themselves decided was fair . . . Churlish as it may seem to complain about administrative benevolence, there is a big constitutional principle at stake. Defective Finance Acts passed by the House of Commons should be put right by the House of Commons, at whose door the blame really lies.

'The U-turn now executed by their Lordships is more than a mere change of mind. It illustrates the renaissance of administrative law in this country which has taken place in the past 20 years . . . The whole picture has been transformed, and for this the public should be profoundly grateful.'

J.P.W.B. McAuslan, Professor of Law at the University of Warwick, was quick to reply: 'Professor Wade's letter beggars belief. It would be difficult to imagine a proposition more calculated to cause a widespread revulsion against the whole notion of government under law than that the public ought to be profoundly grateful that the House of Lords has overturned one of their own decisions of 32 years standing in order to allow the Vestey family to enjoy all the considerable benefits of living in this country without having to contribute a penny piece of income tax towards the preservation of those benefits and this country.'

An error common to many a comment was that the main purpose of the Vestey tax avoidance scheme was to allow the Vestey business to prosper. The statement by Taki in the *Spectator* on October 11, 1980, was typical of this view. 'If the Vestey empire did not use the tax loophole, it would not have been able to maximise its growth, plough back its profits in order to expand, employ more people and pay better salaries.' This parallels the defence which the Vesteys themselves offered for their tax avoidance scheme. After the *Sunday Times* articles Edmund Vestey gave an interview to his local newspaper, the *Saffron Walden Weekly News*. Edmund Vestey said that the family had been faced with a choice of going bankrupt or 'shifting out'. The Vesteys had opted for an intricate system of overseas trusts which, for the past sixty years, had allowed them to plough profits back into their companies.

'If it had not been for the foresight of my grandfather and his brother we would not be where we are today,' Mr Vestey said. 'I have no idea how much the trusts have saved us, but what it has meant is that most of the profits we earn are earned overseas. We have been able to put back in what we have been able to earn. We have been able to compete with foreign competitors because of what our ancestors were able to arrange.'

It is true that much of the Vesteys' profit is made overseas.

From there whatever the business needs for expansion is indeed ploughed back into the empire. But the money paid to the family trust – the £960,000 annual rent, and the dividends from the three offshore companies – does not go back into the business. It ends up in the pockets of various Vesteys for their own personal use. The statement by the Inland Revenue special commissioners to the High Court – not contested by the Vesteys – lists the £2.6 million paid to various Vesteys from the family trust between 1962 and 1966 and then specifically says, 'The above mentioned sums were paid in cash and the proceeds were invested by the recipients *otherwise than in companies in the Vestey family group*' (author's emphasis).

This is a convenient point to consider the issues raised in the Lords' decision and in readers' letters and to suggest ways in which British tax laws might be reformed. It is clear from the reaction to the *Sunday Times* articles on the Vesteys' tax-avoiding schemes that although, legally, there is a very fine line between tax evasion and tax avoidance, in the public's view the two are totally different. Evasion is regarded as improper, dishonest and reprehensible. (Witness the almost universal condemnation of the Fleet Street print workers who were exposed in 1979 as having evaded tax on casual shifts by signing for wages with names like 'Mickey Mouse' and 'Lester Piggott', with appropriate false addresses.) On the other hand tax *avoidance* is generally considered – as the reaction of the *Sunday Times* readers showed – to be a sign of great success, perspicacity and skill, and is widely admired and envied. Yet, of the two, tax avoidance is the far greater problem.

The taxation system in most industrialised countries is a progressive one, based on the principle that those citizens who have a greater ability to pay tax should shoulder a proportionately greater share of the tax bill. But in our society the very people with the greater ability to pay tax are also those who can afford to engage professional experts to find ways of avoiding doing so. This is one reason for the extremely high marginal rates of taxation at the top end of the scale – they are calculated on the assumption that a lot of citizens liable to pay in theory, will in practice legally avoid doing so.

The cost of this avoidance is then shifted on to those less able to pay. The businessman who has spent a lot of money on professional advisers for a tax avoidance scheme passes on the bill to the public in the form of increased prices for goods and services. The cost of the Inland Revenue staff needed to detect and to counter tax avoidance is passed on to the public in the form of increased taxation to pay for this additional public expenditure. And does it really make economic sense to employ highly-skilled professionals – on opposing sides of the tax avoidance line – to engage in such unproductive activity? The twelve-year-long Vestey case involving at enormous cost teams of accountants, solicitors, barristers, judges, Revenue investigators and commissioners – plus all their support staff – is a perfect example of wasteful, unproductive use of skilled and intelligent manpower.

What can be done about it? In the April, 1981 Finance Bill the Chancellor moved to deal with the gap in the tax laws that had worried the Law Lords in the Vestey case. From March 10, 1981 (Budget Day), any UK resident who received money from an overseas trust, whether he was the person who originally transferred the assets to set up the trust, or a later beneficiary, would be taxed, but only on the money *he actually received*. No amount of income would be taken into account more than once in charging tax, both under previous laws and the new ones.

But this is still only tinkering with the main problem. In 1978 Anthony Thompson, then a lecturer in law at Reading

University, suggested a wider approach. Thompson put forward proposals for taxation reform which, although greeted with derision and hostility at the time, now appear remarkably prescient (other countries are successfully working similar schemes and the Treasury has been examining them). At its simplest, what Thompson suggested was one all-embracing anti-tax-avoidance law in which the *intention* of the taxpayer would be paramount. Thompson admits that intention is notoriously difficult to prove in all areas of law, but said that it can be done by the use of inference from proven facts.

'Some guides to the proof of intention might be not only the actual effect of a particular action, but also its reasonably likely and probable effect,' Thompson wrote. 'An intention (whether admitted or inferred) to avoid tax might be a useful starting point. A scheme might therefore be impermissible if its sole, main, or dominant purpose was the avoidance of tax.' Thompson says that this would require further qualification because even the simple act of buying a house might be undertaken to avoid tax, even though this might be the result Parliament intended. 'But there are other schemes which do not have the same innocuous character. One connecting factor may be that the schemes are not *normal* in the sense that their means or nature might not in ordinary human intercourse or ordinary business circumstances be employed to achieve the apparent object, or that they may have created rights and obligations which would not normally be created between parties dealing at arms' length in a transaction of that nature.' Thompson envisaged then, as a starting point for a new anti-avoidance law, a provision incorporating the concepts of intention, effect, arms' length relationship, and normality.

Similar provisions already exist in Germany and the United States. In Germany, if there is a normal method of carrying out a transaction, the citizen is taxed as though this method has been adopted – unless he can prove some legitimate reason, other than tax avoidance, for departing from the norm. In the United States, judges are inclined to look at the taxpayer's position before he embarks on some scheme and compare it with his position afterwards. If it appears that the only purpose of the scheme was to avoid tax, then the American judges would probably rule that the scheme should be ignored and only the reality considered. There was some movement in this direction in Britain in March, 1981, when the House of Lords – *W. T. Ramsay v Inland Revenue* – decided that judges hearing tax avoidance cases were entitled to see beyond a whole series of deals and judge the overall effect.

In 1973, W. T. Ramsay, a farming company, bought a ready-made tax avoidance scheme from a company which specialised in tax planning, enabling them to avoid corporation or capital gains tax. The Inland Revenue refused to recognise the scheme and the case was fought to the House of Lords. There the Crown contended that the scheme, although legal in itself, was a sham and should simply be regarded as artificial. Counsel for Ramsay argued that it did not matter that the motive for a transaction was to avoid tax; unless a specific law banned that transaction, then it was valid.

The Law Lords said that while the techniques of tax avoidance progressed, the courts were not obliged to stand still. Capital gains tax was created to operate in the real world, not that of make-belief. They were impressed by an American decision (*Gilbert v Internal Revenue Commissioner*) where the judge said, 'The Income Tax Act imposes liabilities upon taxpayers based on their financial transactions . . . If, however, the taxpayer enters into a transaction that does not appreciably affect his beneficial interest except to reduce his tax, the law will disregard it.' Lord Wilberforce decided that

Ramsay's scheme was designed to return all the parties within a few days to the position from which they started, and to produce for Ramsay neither gain nor loss. Therefore it was a pure tax avoidance scheme and could be ignored. So he and his four fellow Lords found for the Inland Revenue.

The Revenue's satisfaction at this outcome grew when a similar case, *Furniss v Dawson*, came before the House of Lords three years later. The Furniss family, to avoid capital gains tax on share sales, had embarked on a series of transactions ending in the Isle of Man where there was no tax liability. The Law Lords found that since the family's purpose was clear, they could disregard the first transaction in the series and the Inland Revenue could levy the tax. Taken together the two cases were thought by some authorities to be the most important for tax law this century, but in practice they have not produced the effect the Inland Revenue hoped. One tax accountant commented, 'The principle which the Ramsay and Furniss cases appeared to establish has been somewhat eroded as the Revenue has tried, perhaps too hard, to press home its advantage.'

So we are back to Thompson's view that the proliferation each year of legislation to try to stop tax avoidance, and of expensive and time-consuming tax cases, can only be halted by a radically new approach. His conclusion is as apt for the Vestey affair as it is for his own proposals: 'Positive action now might enable us to have a simpler, fairer and more intelligible tax system with lower rates of tax for all. It may even be possible to restore our tax laws from the pillory to a position of pride and respect.'

11

The Australian End

Uproar as the aborigines fight back

The Vesteys went to Australia just before the First World War and were quick to see the opportunities there. In some ways it was like Argentina: vast areas of unexploited land, a small population, and large numbers of animals used mainly for a product other than meat. Just as the Argentinians regarded cattle primarily as a source of leather, so Australians looked on sheep mainly as a source of wool. The Vesteys' first interest in Australia, therefore, was as a source of cheap mutton. But then they were offered a marvellous opportunity. The Labour government of 1910–13 took over control of the Northern Territory, the least developed part of Australia, and prepared plans to exploit it by granting cheap leases to resident small landowners. It sent a team of experts to the Territory's largest town, Darwin, to head a new administration, with orders to implement the development plan as soon as possible.

Unfortunately the government chose as its administrator Dr J.A. Gilruth, an Aberdeen Scot of extreme conservative views. The government had envisaged leasing land on perpetual tenure providing the occupier developed it. They wanted resident pastoralists (ranchers) who would take an interest in the area, and they planned to build a state-sponsored packing plant at Darwin to process the cattle raised on these small, owner-occupied properties. Gilruth saw differently. He believed that the quickest way to develop the Territory was to invite a large company that already had the expertise, to start a beef industry from scratch, and that to attract such a company the terms would have to be generous. These views coincided with those of the conservative government which replaced Labour in 1913.

So Gilruth was able to offer the Vesteys a very favourable deal: huge tracts of land on long leases at peppercorn rents. After Evelyn Brodstone had rushed to Australia to examine the proposition, the Vesteys accepted. Between 1914 and 1916 they leased 36,000 square miles of pastoral land in the Northern Territory and the East Kimberley district of Western Australia. (This is an area larger than the state of Tasmania and one third the size of New Zealand.) The rent was unbelievably low, and remained so for many years. For example, in 1980 for their Wave Hill station in the Northern Territory the Vesteys were paying for its 6,158 square miles – an area about equal in size to the English Midlands – a rent of 55 cents (27p) per sq. mile per year. Or, expressed in terms better understood in Britain, for a cattle farm of nearly four million acres they were paying an annual rent of about £1,650.

The Vesteys also built a packing plant at Darwin, the one which the Labour government had originally proposed to build itself. They opened the plant in 1917, closed it in 1920, then allowed it to fall into disuse. When they first closed it, the Vesteys blamed 'labour indiscipline' and the poor quality of the local cattle. As a result, by 1927 exports of cattle from the Northern Territory were lower than at any time since the turn of the century. What had gone wrong? Australian historian J.H. Kelly offers a theory. He says that the Vesteys became concerned that Australian beef would prove a powerful competitor in Britain for the Vesteys' much more profitable South American operations, especially since the Vesteys were sufficiently far-sighted to realise that some form of empire preference was inevitable. But if the Vesteys had turned down the offer from the Australian government to build a packing plant at Darwin there would have been the risk that someone else would have accepted, or that any future Labour government would have resurrected the idea of a State-owned plant. So by being prepared to invest £1 million to build a packing plant and then not run it, the Vesteys stopped Australian beef from competing with South American and, at the same time, made sure that no one else could compete with them in Australia.

But other historians deny this. They say that the Australian government failed to keep its part of the deal with the Vesteys – that it would build a railway between Alice Springs and Darwin so as to bring cattle to the packing plant. This not only meant that the plant could not operate profitably, it also forced the Vesteys to send their own cattle to abattoirs on the Queensland coast. Droving them in mobs of 1,000 to 1,500 head was the only means of doing this. These cattle drives sometimes took three years – ten miles a day was considered good progress – and became part of the romantic outback legend of Australia, a subject for books and films in which the drover was the archetypal folk hero. In this disagreement between Australian historians it is hard to decide who is right.

The Vesteys' plans in Darwin certainly met with opposition from locals, largely from the infant Northern Territory Workers' Union (NTWU), which suspected strong links between Gilruth, the administrator, and the Vesteys. Gilruth had gone to London in 1919 for consultations with William and Edmund. On his return, John Carey, a man he had originally brought with him from Melbourne as his private secretary and who had since become Director of Lands, Director of Agriculture, Chief Protector of Aborigines, Chief Censor, and Acting Administrator in Gilruth's absence, also took the job as chief clerk at the Vestey packing plant. The NTWU complained to Gilruth that this involved a conflict of interests so profound that it was scandalous, but Gilruth refused to accept the complaint or to forward it to the authorities in the Federal capital.

The NTWU now believed that the Vesteys and the administrator would thwart any attempt to have an independent inquiry into the Vestey operation in the Northern Territory so the union decided to take matters into its own hands. A typist in the Vesteys' office provided the weapon. Carey, wearing his hat as the Vesteys' chief clerk, gave her a letter to type. It was addressed to the Vesteys in Smithfield. Historian H.I. Jensen, in *The Darwin Rebellion*, describes its contents. 'It stated that the lease of a large pastoral holding with hundreds of thousands of head of cattle on it would expire shortly. The Administrator could refuse renewal and grant it to the Vesteys, but it would be necessary to pay him £20,000 to use as graft for officials and parliament for this purpose.'

A copy of the letter 'found its way' to the NTWU which

called a meeting of the Darwin council whose chairman, coincidentally, was none other than John Carey. At a stormy meeting the council carried a vote of no-confidence in Carey, another motion deposing Gilruth as administrator, Carey as Government Secretary, and the Territory's judge and the official accountant for good measure. A further motion ordered all these officials to leave Darwin by the next steamer, and announced that until a new administrator arrived, the Northern Territory would be run by the council. The contents of Carey's letter to the Vesteys and all the council's motions were telegraphed to the Prime Minister, William Hughes, a general strike was declared, and meatworkers marched on the Vestey packing plant demanding Carey's sacking. The third and last rebellion against constitutional authority in Australia had begun.*

The Federal government's reaction was to order a warship, HMAS *Melbourne*, to steam at full speed to Darwin to maintain order. When it arrived Gilruth was smuggled on board and the ship sailed soon afterwards, the captain reporting that his crew were becoming sympathetic with the Darwin workers and that he feared for their loyalty. Two days later a Burns Philp steamship took off Carey and the other officials after the captain had been told that if these men remained, the Darwin workers had plans to throw them into the harbour. When the Federal government announced that it would order a Royal Commission, the NTWU called off the strike and the rebellion was over. The commission found that while the Darwin workers had behaved unconstitutionally it was difficult

* The other two were the Rum Rebellion, 1808, and the Eureka Stockade, 1854.

to blame them because 'the confidence of the public in the Commonwealth, and in receiving just, impartial, and humane treatment, was shaken to its foundations' by what had happened.

In the 1930s the Vesteys' interest in Australia was revived. Empire preference became a reality and new technical developments made it possible to transport chilled – rather than the less palatable frozen – beef from Australia to Britain. In January, 1934, the Vesteys took over the Angliss meat interests in Australia for £1.5 million; the largest British-owned concern in the trade had gained control of the largest group of meat companies in Australia. By the mid-thirties the Australian meat export trade was almost entirely in the hands of overseas groups – the Vesteys, the Borthwicks, and the Swifts.

A new Labour government felt that this was unacceptable and commissioned the Payne–Fletcher report, 'Development in the North'. Published in 1937, the report said that the entire north-western section of the Northern Territory was in large holdings controlled by three companies: the Northern Agency Ltd (the Vesteys), Bovril Australian Estates Ltd, and Connor, Doherty and Durack Ltd. All held long leases at low rents without improvement or development conditions, and enjoyed generous concessions by way of cheap freight and subsidies for structural improvements.

Payne and Fletcher said that these properties were 'too large to be developed to their full capacity under one control and management'. They advocated the breaking up of large holdings, their replacement with moderate-sized properties under long and secure tenure, and a wide extension of the railway network. The Labour government fell the following year, but the new Minister for the Interior, John McEwen, was committed to the development of the north and saw the force of the Payne–Fletcher proposals. He promised to draw up a five-year plan for road and rail development and to review all leases with a view to resuming those where the occupiers' performance had not been in the best interests of the area. But war broke out before this could be done, McEwen was transferred to the Defence Department, and none of the Payne–Fletcher proposals were implemented.

In 1945, a new Labour government established a North Australia Development Committee which largely repeated the Payne–Fletcher criticism: 'the committee considers that it is better to have a number of resident leases on areas of reasonable and adequate size than to have very large areas leased to non-resident companies . . . Without an adequate railway system the development of northern Australia cannot succeed.' By 1949 the Labour government was ready to implement the reforms recommended by Payne–Fletcher and the Development Committee, but it was defeated in the elections of that year and the climate of urgency for the development of the north changed to one of complacency.

Meanwhile the Vesteys had found a welcome tax loophole in Australian tax laws. In order to encourage primary production in the Northern Territory the Federal government had passed a law which said, in effect, that income derived directly from primary production in the Northern Territory by a resident of that Territory was not subject to income tax. It did not take the Vesteys long to realise that the word 'resident' was not specifically defined. When the Australian Taxation Commissioner assessed them on their income from their properties in the Northern Territory they challenged the assessment in the High Court arguing that they were, in effect, residents. They operated there, they had houses there. The High Court upheld the Vestey appeal and for fifteen years – 1937 until 1952 when the loophole was closed – the Vesteys and every other non-resident pastoral company in the Northern Territory enjoyed their corporate income from their activities there free of income tax.

In 1954 the Vesteys' leaseholds in the Northern Territory were renewed for a further fifty years. Until the renewal date the Vesteys held 30,758 square miles of Northern Territory land. In return for renewal of the major part of this until 2004 they agreed to surrender 13,700 square miles of land. But, according to J.H. Kelly, more than 10,000 square miles of this surrendered land was of inferior quality. The Darwin newspaper, the *Darwin Standard*, said at the time that under the renewal conditions the Vesteys were not obliged to make any structural improvements such as buildings and stockyards, they were required to erect only 510 miles of fencing – just over 10 miles a year – and to sink only 39 watering holes.

The Vesteys pressed on. In 1964 the Northern Territory Pastoral Lessees' Association, of which the Vesteys were leading members, proposed to the Australian government that it should change the leases held by absentee pastoralists to freehold titles. The then Minister for Territories, C.E. Barnes, announced that he approved this proposal and would be introducing legislation to implement it. This announcement caused such an uproar throughout Australia that the government had to abandon its plans.

The vehemence of the public reaction was due partly to a new sense of nationalism in Australia which resented the dominance of overseas interests in the Australian cattle industry and partly to a guilty conscience over the treatment of aborigines and their tribal lands, which were often on leases granted to the pastoralists.

In the early days of the Vestey operation in Australia they, like most of the other pastoralists, did not pay their aboriginal workmen any wages at all, providing only accommodation and food. There is a story in anthropological circles that a researcher on one Vestey station listened to an aboriginal stockman describe an epic overland cattle drive that had lasted many months and yet had been completed with minimum loss of cattle. The researcher asked whether the Vestey manager had shown his appreciation by giving the stockman some form of bonus. The aborigine was puzzled until the word bonus was explained to him, then his face lit up. 'Yes, boss,' he said. 'They gave me a bag of lollies.'

It was not until the twenties that the conditions for aborigines began to cause some concern, and in 1929 the publication of a report by J.W. Bleakley on the welfare of aborigines in the Northern Territory emphasised how bad things were. Bleakley, a man not easily shocked by the pastoralists' treatment of aboriginal workmen – he was Protector of Aborigines in the state of Queensland, not the most enlightened state in Australia – was scathing about the Vesteys and other pastoralists. He said that the accommodation provided on some stations (ranches) consisted of iron huts that were little better than dog kennels. Aged dependants of the workmen were often starving and no station manager thought it necessary to make even the most rudimentary provision for educating the stockmen's children, arguing that education would only make them 'cunning and cheeky'. Bleakley wrote,

'The trouble probably is that they become enlightened and as a result dissatisfied with their conditions.'

Bleakley's main conclusion was that the first step towards proper working conditions for aborigines was that they should be paid a living wage. He argued that it was in the pastoralists' own interests to do this because they were absolutely dependent on aboriginal labour and their claim that they could not afford to pay wages was false because some pastoralists were already doing so and were prospering. Implied, but not stated, in his report was the reason for the reluctance of most pastoralists to pay wages. Many, including the Vesteys, had found that the best way of managing a station when you were an absentee owner was to put the station manager on a sliding salary linked to the cost of running the station. On a Vestey station, instead of getting a bonus if profits were good, the manager received increases if he kept costs down, and the lower the costs, the greater his increase.

When the Bleakley report was published, the Commonwealth Minister for Home Affairs called a conference in Melbourne to discuss it. Participants included religious groups which had mission stations in the area, aboriginal welfare organisations, anthropological societies, and the Northern Territory Pastoral Lessees' Association. The Association made it clear that it would not accept Bleakley's recommendation for paying wages to aborigines and it took political steps to block any move to do this. The welfare groups, lacking the power of the association, retreated and it was sixteen years before there was another official look at conditions for aboriginal stockmen.

It was the Vesteys who initiated this. By 1946 they were the major employer of aboriginal labour in the Northern Territory and they were having trouble in finding sufficient aboriginal stockmen willing to work for them. The Vesteys decided to seek advice from experts and contacted the anthropology department of Sydney University asking for its help. The department gave the job to the husband and wife team, Dr Ronald and Catherine Berndt. They wrote to the Vesteys setting out what they would need for their preliminary research: access to company records, permission to visit the properties and to inspect conditions. The Vesteys immediately invoked their customary claim to privacy with the same speed William had shown when the Joint Commission on the Argentine Meat Trade wanted to inspect the Vestey company records in London.

They replied that they did not see how this could be relevant: the company books would show nothing about the shortage of stockmen; they were well aware of conditions on their own properties and did not need to be advised about them. The Berndts wrote that what the Vesteys really wanted was for them to 'contact the bush natives and endeavour to settle them somewhere on their stations where they would be able more or less to keep them in hand and utilise the labour that was suitable.'

The Berndts noted that there had been a steady decline in the number of aborigines willing to work on many stations, as predicted by Bleakley many years earlier. The Vesteys had not noticed this trend, however, because of a slow drift northwards of the desert tribes who had filled the gaps in the labour ranks. It was only when the desert tribes appeared to be dying out that the Vesteys had been forced to try other recruitment techniques.

First the Berndts went into the general history of the relationship between pastoralists and aborigines. In some cases they found that each side had received what it had wanted: the pastoralists had sought faithful and competent service for the lowest possible cost and the aborigines had been prepared to provide this – as long as they felt inclined – in return for the novel goods introduced by the white man. But in other cases, the relationship had been much more coercive: in the last century one tribe which had been reluctant to work and had taken to spearing cattle because they were on the tribe's traditional hunting ground was nearly exterminated; in other areas aborigines who left the station were classed as 'runaways' and were forcibly returned by the police.

When they came to inspect the Vestey stations, the Berndts could hardly believe what they saw. The aborigines lived in crudely-built shacks of old bagging and iron. These were rarely waterproof and would disintegrate in a strong wind. Sanitation and rubbish disposal were virtually non-existent. There was scarcely any access to potable water. On one station night soil was dumped in an area used to catch water in the wet season. Although the white man's drinking water was filtered or came from tank rainwater, the aborigines were refused permission to use even the station garden hose to replenish their own supplies. The working day had no limits and depended on the inclination of the employer. Children were allocated various functions from an early age even though the government *Aboriginals Ordinance* prohibited the employment of those under twelve. The Vestey management attitude was 'catch them young and train them'.

If the station needed any extra labour, the management would call on men from the tribal camp, irrespective of whether they had any employment arrangement with them. These men were seldom entered in the official returns to the Department of Native Affairs, were not therefore classed as 'employed natives' and so had no right to the official wage of five shillings a week. Medical attention was spasmodic, insufficient, often unskilled and inappropriate. During their visit to the Vesteys' Wave Hill station, the Berndts recorded the births of three children and another was born soon after they left. Only one of the four survived.

Food usually consisted of 'a hunk of dry bread, a piece of cooked beef, and a pannikin of sweetened tea' three times a day for each working man and woman. Aged and infirm dependants received infrequently a small helping of flour, some sugar with a sprinkling of tea leaves, soap and tobacco. As an occasional treat they were also given 'mouldy jam or weevilly porridge' thrown out of the company store as being unfit for European consumption. When someone at the station slaughtered a beast the aborigines were given the offal and unwanted bones. In the case of women employed in or about the station house there was the valuable 'right' to scraps of kitchen garbage. Permanent workers were provided with dresses, shirts, trousers, sweaters, combs, mirrors and handkerchiefs at infrequent intervals. These and their frugal food and tobacco issue were the aborigines' total reward for their labour.

The Berndts decided that employers generally in the Northern Territory had taken advantage of the sociological fact that in their natural habitat the aborigines regarded the possession of personal property of any sort as a physical handicap. The employers argued, therefore, that what they gave the aborigines for their labours was more than ample. As a result the aborigines reached the end of their working life with nothing to show for their labour. They were then forced to exist on the station manager's charity.

The Berndts found that on some Vestey stations, the

aboriginal women supplemented their rations by prostitution. White women were not encouraged to live on the stations because the company was reluctant to bear the additional cost of providing satisfactory accommodation for them. The Berndts found that at one Vestey station girls as young as seven had been taken into the traffic ostensibly to assist Europeans to avoid venereal disease.

Over a period of time, the Berndts made a series of recommendations to the Vesteys for improving the conditions of the aborigines and introducing a small cash wage. The company was at first incensed by the idea that any improvements were needed and it rejected out of hand any idea of a wage. Its reply read, 'We are opposed to the payment of wages to natives, and consider that there has been enough trouble with wage systems. Money seems to be the root of all evil.'

The Berndts' conclusion is worth quoting at length. '[Vesteys] are anxious to retain the *status quo* – at least as far as they can manage it. They resent any interference with "their natives" and look on Government regulations as unjust and annoying red tape to be circumvented wherever possible. Some [managers] on these stations, as on others, actively dislike the aborigines and express indifference or positive pleasure at the thought of their ultimate extinction. Here were evident the same tendencies that marked the control of white workers in Europe in the nineteenth century, before the sweating of labour for quick profits began to give way to more enlightened tactics. In both cases there were assumptions that workers were plentiful, that it was unnecessary to worry about the future supply.'

The Berndts remarked on how the white Australians on Vestey stations used the fear of force to maintain discipline. 'In February 1946 three young men were caught trying to make off with a few cattle. They were chained up at the homestead for several days and severely beaten to "teach them a lesson". We were assured that such incidents were required fairly frequently, because "you've got to keep the niggers in their place".' (No doubt a similar attitude existed on other stations. Before aboriginal citizenship in 1967, those living on cattle stations were classified as 'inmates of institutions' and generally treated as such.)

The Berndts' report was published in 1948, 'A Northern Territory Problem: Aboriginal Labour in a Pastoral Area.' But it was not until 1957 that there was some improvement. In that year, the weekly wage for an adult aboriginal stockman was fixed at A$4.85 (about £2.40) with keep. Two years later it was raised by a clothing allowance of A$1.50 (75p) making a total of less than one-fifth the wage of a white stockman. It is not known how many aborigines actually received this wage because the Welfare Branch of the Northern Territory Administration at that time had never taken action against any station owner or manager for non-payment of aboriginal wages, despite frequent allegations that employers were ignoring the new rates.

In 1965, the full bench of the Arbitration Commission, the body in Australia which fixes workers' wages and conditions, heard an application from the North Australian Workers' Union asking for an end to wage discrimination against aborigines employed in the Northern Territory pastoral industry. Opposition to the application was led by the Northern Territory Pastoral Lessees' Association and the Northern Territory Cattle Producers' Council, both of which were dominated by the Vestey management. Principal witness for the council was the Vesteys' pastoral superintendent in Northern Australia, Peter Morris. The Vesteys did not resist demands for reform, but they argued for delay. To give the aborigines an 'artificial' high wage now, rather than a gradual increase, would do more harm than good. This argument was accepted. The commission ruled that wage discrimination would have to end but it allowed the Vesteys and other pastoralists three years to bring the aborigines up to the white worker levels and left a loophole: the employer did not have to pay the full rate to any aborigine classed as a 'slow worker'.

By now a new generation of aboriginal workers were becoming increasingly aware of their rights and their power. But, ironically, the most important factor in what now occurred had its origins in the attitude of the pastoralists themselves. By denying their aboriginal workers access to living conditions enjoyed by white Australians and by keeping them outside the cash economy, the pastoralists had unwittingly forced the aborigines to maintain their traditional lifestyle. So, although slow to anger and not prone to carry resentment for long, when they nevertheless felt by the mid-1960s that they had had enough, they were still sufficiently outside of and independent from the pastoralists' world to take the dramatic step of going on strike. At stations all over the Northern Territory, in unorganised and uncoordinated protest, aboriginal stockmen simply walked off the job. Most of these protests received little or no publicity, but one strike became national news.

On August 23, 1966, Vincent Lingiari led 200 members of his Gurindji tribe off the Vesteys' Wave Hill cattle station. Lingiari died in 1984, but one of the stockmen, Bill Bunter Jampijinpa, recalls: 'We were fed up. We were treated just like dogs. We were lucky to get paid the fifty quid a month we were due, and we lived in tin humpies you had to crawl in and out of on your knees. There was no running water. The food was bad – just flour, tea, sugar and bits of beef like the head or feet of a bullock. The Vestey mob were hard men. They didn't care about black fellas.'

This assessment was confirmed by journalist Christopher Forsyth who wrote in *The Australian* at the time: 'The accommodation provided by the Vesteys for the aborigines was rusted iron shells, four walls leaning towards each other, pieces of hessian covering the worst holes. There were twenty-five of them . . . none was higher than four feet with an opening of about three feet six inches. They were about five feet wide and eight feet long. There appeared to be no water and certainly no sanitation. I had never seen a more desolate place, nor such a disgusting sight in a country which prides itself in giving people a fair go.' Author Frank Hardy, who later helped publicise the strike, adds: 'It was a pitiful sight . . . no floors, no water taps, no toilets, no laundry facilities, no wood, no beds, no furniture – nothing except a few pathetic heaps of rags, tattered blankets and old clothes in each hut, and here and there a rusty tin plate or a picture of Jesus pasted on the wall.'

Jampijinpa remembers how the protest began: 'Old Vincent came back from hospital in Darwin and said he had decided that he would pull us out. He pulled everyone out that Tuesday and we walked with the kids and our swags to the Victoria River and set up camp there. After we'd been there a couple of days the Vestey mob came and said they would get two killers (slaughtered beasts] and raise our wages if we came back. Old Vincent said, "No, we're stopping here." So we stayed there until the New Year and then we walked to our new promised land, we call it Daguragu, back to our sacred places and our country, our new homeland.'

This apparently minor incident in a remote part of

the Northern Territory is now recognised as marking the beginning of the aboriginal land rights movement, perhaps the most significant event in Australian history since the various states banded together to form the Commonwealth in 1901. The point was that 'Daguragu' was known to white Australians as Wattie Creek and it was within the boundaries of the Vesteys' Wave Hill station. The Gurindji, Vestey employees, were claiming Vestey land.

They announced that they wanted to start a co-operative venture to catch and break in wild horses and contract their services to the Vesteys for cattle mustering, fencing, branding and other station work. But under Australian law the aborigines were squatters and the Vesteys would have been within their legal rights in ordering the aborigines to leave and, if they refused, in forcing them to do so. But by now the aborigines' stand had caught the attention of the metropolitan media, and trade union, church, student and writers' organisations moved in to lend the aborigines their support. The emotional appeal of the aborigines' case was strong, as an incident described by Frank Hardy illustrates. Peter Morris, the Vesteys' superintendent who was the principal witness in the Arbitration Commission case against giving the aborigines equal pay, approached Vincent Lingiari and demanded, 'What are you doing on Vesteys' land?' Vincent thought for a moment and then replied, 'I dunno. This belong to my grandfather.'

So the Vesteys did not force the issue. They pointed out, correctly, that they only *leased* the land from the Federal government and it was not for them to decide whether the aborigines' claim that it was tribal land was correct. They said that they were prepared to co-operate in any solution the government proposed, including making land which they held under government lease available to the Gurindji.

Encouraged by this announcement and the support they were getting from groups in metropolitan Australia, the aborigines submitted to the government a request for 500 square miles of Wave Hill's 6,158 square miles of land, claiming that it was tribal territory. At one stage their prospects looked good. The government of the day, the Liberal-Country Party coalition, had said that it favoured policies to help the aborigines help themselves and the Minister for Aboriginal Affairs, W.C. Wentworth, had shown sympathy with the Wave Hill strikers' claim.

But when the matter came to a Cabinet decision two main factors were instrumental in crushing the aborigines' hopes. The first was a political one. The Country Party section of the coalition relied for its support on protecting the interests of established landowners and these landowners saw the Wave Hill strike, the Wattie Creek squat, and the claim for aboriginal land rights as dangerous precedents. The second was an economic one. Australia was in the middle of a minerals boom. There appeared to be no limit to the extent and nature of mineral discovery. If the government recognised aboriginal land rights and then an enormous mineral strike was made on tribal land, what would happen? Despite Wentworth's efforts on behalf of the Wattie Creek aborigines – he broke Cabinet solidarity to express publicly his disappointment – the Cabinet rejected their claim and said it was not in favour of granting land rights to aborigines. The finality of this decision appeared confirmed when another group of aborigines lost a High Court action against a mining company, the judge, Mr Justice Blackburn, reaching the interesting conclusion that 'the aborigines belong to the land more than the land belongs to the aborigines.'

Then the outlook brightened. In December, 1972, the Australian Labour Party was returned to power after twenty years in Opposition. There is ample evidence that the failure of the Liberal-Country Party government to live up to the expectations of the Australian people on the question of aboriginal affairs played an important part in that victory. The new government announced that it would reverse the trend of 200 years of 'despoliation, injustice, and discrimination which have seriously damaged and demoralised the once proud aboriginal people'.

The Vesteys had already made their own views clear. Lord Vestey had been in Australia on business earlier in 1972 and had been asked about the aboriginal demands and Labour Party policy. First he fired a blast at city-dwelling Australians, specifically aimed at those who had supported the Gurindjis at Wave Hill. 'The trouble with Melbourne people is that they have never been to the Northern Territory,' he said. 'You killed all your abos [in Victoria]. Now you have a guilt complex and you meddle in things you don't understand. All the trouble about the Northern Territory abos is stirred up by communists and the Melbourne papers. People down here wouldn't know a Gurindji from a Wailbri.' The he became more conciliatory and offered a reasonable analysis of the situation. He said, 'The aboriginal problem is very serious. We do employ a lot of aborigines, but not as many as we used to, because cattle breeding is becoming more highly-mechanised now. But the aboriginal problem can't be solved in little pockets. It's a national problem which must be solved on a national scale. We are quite concerned and prepared to talk about the problem and in our own way we are doing all we can about it. But letting aborigines own land and the whole thing about tribal and sacred land are two different things. It cannot possibly be any government's policy to invite overseas companies to raise beef or what have you and then tell them they can't use the land because it is sacred to aborigines.'

The Labour government went ahead with its plans and in 1975 gave the Gurindjis 2,000 square kilometres of tribal land from the Vesteys' leases. The then Prime Minister, Gough Whitlam, went to Daguragu and poured a handful of soil through Vincent Lingiari's hands in a symbolic reversal of the aborigines' giving of earth to the British settler John Batman in 1834 for the handover of the land that is now Melbourne.

But within months Whitlam's government was swept from office and the Liberal-Country Party coalition returned to power. Although Whitlam's land rights legislation for the Northern Territory was enacted in amended form, the new government confirmed its general policy: it was against granting automatic land rights to all aborigines.

The Vesteys acted quickly to improve conditions at Wave Hill, spending A$1 million (about £500,000) on a modernisation programme. This included new quarters for aboriginal stockmen that became a model for the rest of the Northern Territory. And they increased wages steadily until they reached $160 (about £80) a week, less $35 for keep. But the Australasian Meat Industry Employees Union reported that there had been a deep-seated change in aboriginal attitudes. 'They will no longer tolerate the racial abuse handed out by most managers and head stockmen. This abuse has been a common factor in all the disputes of which we heard. The result of their stand? They are no longer offered jobs.'

For the next ten years it became difficult to get an accurate picture of what was happening with aborigines on Vestey cattle stations in Australia. The stations were remote, isolated and visitors were allowed only with prior permission. Journalists, union officials and members of aboriginal support groups were not welcome. Government officials and pastoralists maintained secrecy about their operations. Frank Stevens* gives two examples. When the Labour government was still in power he was instructed by the Minister for Aboriginal Affairs, Gordon Bryant, to help prepare the Commonwealth's brief for the hearing in the Arbitration Commission of the *Cattle Station Industry (Northern Territory) Award*. In order to obtain precise information on operating costs, wage rates, and capitalisation of cattle properties, Stevens approached the Department of Aboriginal Affairs for cost-benefit analyses of typical cattle stations. Stevens knew it would be unlikely that the department would have such information about any of the leading pastoralists – as we have seen, the Vesteys would certainly not have given these figures to any government department – but the Labour government was in the process of buying some cattle stations for aborigines and Stevens argued that it must have seen cost-benefit analyses for these stations. He received no answer to his request.

Later he asked the same department for photographs of the conditions of aborigines on cattle stations. Stevens said he had convinced the Minister that these photographs would be of great value, not only for legal reasons, but

* Stevens, associate professor of industrial relations at the University of New South Wales, was instrumental in bringing the working conditions of aborigines to public notice. He is the author of *The Politics of Prejudice*, Alternative Publishing Co-operative, Sydney, 1980.

for an historical record, and that the Minister had agreed that his department should provide them. Stevens says that although the Northern Territory branch of the department agreed to co-operate, he never received any photographs. When he pressed the matter, the Department replied that it felt the taking of photographs would upset the pastoralists. Stevens says, 'The reaction of the department can only be described as obstructionist.'

Because the Vesteys were in the public eye at the time of the Wave Hill strike, some news of conditions on other Vestey properties occasionally surfaced. It was clear that the Vestey response – and that of other pastoralists – to equal wage legislation had been to cut their aboriginal workforce, sometimes by as much as three-quarters.

The Vestey property known as Gordon Downs in the Kimberley, a remote region in the north of Western Australia, covered almost a million acres and was leased from the Australian government for about $1,000 a year (about £500). In January 1979 the Kimberley Aboriginal Land Council complained about conditions at Gordon Downs to Dr Herbert Combs, formerly the Governor of the Reserve Bank of Australia, one-time Chancellor of the Australian National University, and a campaigner for aboriginal rights. Coombs then wrote to Lord Vestey in London setting out his concern at what was happening at Gordon Downs. The problem seemed to have arisen largely over aborigines who lived on the Vestey property because they said it was their tribal land but for whom the station did not accept any responsibility.

From what Coombs wrote and from a report in *The Observer* by Michael Gillard who visited the station in 1978, it was clear that conditions generally for aborigines were still appalling. Gillard said the station provided nine twenty-foot by twelve-foot one-room iron huts for its aboriginal employees. Other aborigines (who were not, however, employed on the station) lived in 'humpies', low level temporary dwellings which were little more than four feet high and were made from canvas, blankets, or corrugated iron sheets. There was no piped water to the huts, limited electricity, and means of sewage disposal were elementary. Water was supplied to the whole aboriginal camp by one motor-driven pump fifty yards away. A small hut containing showers and latrines was next to the pump. Gillard said that when he visited the station, the pump was not working and aborigines said that they had to carry water from the station manager's house 200 yards away.

The aborigines' health was poor. Professor Fred Hollows, director of the Government-financed National Trachoma and Eye Health Programme, reported after visiting Gordon Downs in June, 1977, 'We had been to some pretty bad places but we were still appalled. There was just one pump. Litter and garbage were everywhere. The people were cramped together living in a few tin huts.' Out of ten aboriginal children under eleven who were examined, eight showed evidence of trachoma, a figure higher than average for other aboriginal communities. Hollows said that bad environmental health, in particular the lack of water, was a major explanation for the high trachoma rate.

Perhaps more disturbing than the conditions for the aborigines was what happened to them (and their dependants not employed on the station) when the Vestey management no longer wanted to employ them. Dr Coombs summed up his view of their predicament: 'The management of the station is deliberately forcing the removal of aborigines from the station which included land with which they and their ancestors have traditional affiliation. This policy is, it is asserted, being made effective by denying all employment opportunities, by refusing access to the station store, by insisting that individual aborigines upon whom others are dependent leave the area, by denying help in relation to social security benefit claims, by referring those in need of medical attention to Hall's Creek, a distance of 120 miles, and by a variety of similar harassments and denials of conventional humanitarian aid.'

Lord Vestey replied in detail to all the complaints about Gordon Downs. It is worthwhile quoting his reply at length. Lord Vestey began by saying that he considered the station manager at Gordon Downs to be a good man 'and we back him one hundred per cent'. Lord Vestey then went on:

'Throughout that area of Australia – not only on our stations – it is normal to have living accommodation which is very basic: a room, a bed, and an ablution block separate from the sleeping quarters. That is fairly standard for aborigines and whites. The normal situation is that there is piped water to the aborigines' ablution block, approximately fifty yards from the living quarters. There are two bores at the station – one for the main settlement and one for the aborigine settlement. Occasionally the aborigines leave the taps running and their bore runs dry.

'It is correct that people – black and white – needing medical treatment are referred to Hall's Creek. They have to make their own way there unless there is an emergency requiring the Flying Doctor. We don't understand why Gordon Downs is being singled out when nearly every pastoral station in Western Australia, Northern Territory, and western Queensland has had five years of appalling economic circumstances and labour forces have had to be cut down all round. We do not believe that our treatment of aborigines is in any way different from anyone else and, in fact, is in our opinion generally better.'

Lord Vestey then went on to deal with the reasons why the aboriginal workforce at Gordon Downs had been cut from forty-four in 1967 to eleven in 1978. 'When the Australian government introduced equal wages in 1967, our company, like others, had to reduce the workforce. We now have at Gordon Downs six permanent aboriginal stockmen with their wives employed as domestics. There are four pensioners and with dependants the total number of aborigines for whom we accept responsibility is about thirty,' Lord Vestey said.

'The difficulty arises because these thirty are joined in a tribal-cum-family way by about 100 relatives and friends, some of whom are nomadic. It is these people who live in the "humpies" while our own people live in accommodation built to the standards laid down by the Australian authorities. We cannot assume responsibility for itinerants, nor are we equipped to do so, nor do we intend to do so. Only our own workers are allowed to use the company store and to cash their social security cheques there. No one else is, black or white.

'Not enough emphasis can be laid on the fact that Gordon Downs is an isolated cattle station and is in no position to cater for large mobile populations which travel unpredictably. We cater for the people employed by the station and employees laid off at the end of the season are assisted in making their social security claims. We do not have the staff to help the itinerants, nor do we carry sufficient cash to cash their cheques.

'It is not true that we are deliberately harassing redundant workers off the stations, but we do hope that when, unfortunately, men have to be made redundant, they will leave. We have had no request from the Australian government to release land for the aborigines, but we are quite prepared to negotiate this, if this is what the government wants us to do.'

Then, in the early 1980s, after seventy years as one of Australia's largest landowners, the Vesteys suddenly began to sell, eventually getting rid of five of their seven Northern Territory stations. The move appeared inexplicable. Apart from their commercial interests in the country, the Vesteys had strong emotional ties: Lord Vestey's mother is Australian, the granddaughter of the great Australian soprano, Dame Nellie Melba, Lord Vestey himself had lived near Melbourne for five years after the war, and three of Lord Vestey's cousins married Australian women while on study tours there. Australia was a finishing school for young Vesteys bound for a career in the family concern, a place where they tested their manhood in the tough and egalitarian world of the Australian working man.

To their credit most passed muster. They worked in the Vestey abattoirs, helping slaughter and butcher the animals, in the family fish processing factory in Western Australia, and on the Vestey cattle stations. When young Mark Vestey, fresh from Eton, stepped off the plane in the Northern Territory to do his spell as a jackaroo, the locals jeered him. Mark walked up to the nearest Australian worker, grabbed a bottle of beer from his hand, bit off the top and downed the beer in two gulps, winning instant recognition. John Vestey rode a motorcycle round the family stations, announcing defiantly, 'I'm a Pommy jackaroo. So what?'

The way the Vesteys ran their stations gave a clear

indication that they had never intended selling. Dr Richard Moneypenny, an Australian agricultural economist, says, 'The Vestey approach to making money in Australia was to minimise their costs. Because the land had been given to them, they didn't expect to make money out of it by selling it, so they didn't bother to improve it. All they did was to harvest cattle. That's pure profit because you've put nothing into it. It was rape of a people, land and country.'

But by the early 1990s, it looked as if by winding down their Australian operation the Vesteys had shown that foresight that had helped their ancestors make the family fortune in the first place. The market for Australian beef had undergone a change, the European market declining, the American and Japanese expanding. The growth of Australian nationalism had started to cause resentment about the level of foreign investment in Australian primary industries (a popular slogan in the Whitlam era was 'Let's buy back the farm'). And in June, 1992 the High Court of Australia, in a shock decision, overturned a legal maxim that had held sway for more than 200 years – that when the British arrived, the country was empty (*terra nullius*), that legally the aborigines did not exist and therefore the Crown had proper title to whatever land it took. After the High Court judgment, maps hastily drawn up in Canberra indicated that only 15 per cent of the country was freehold land owned by ordinary Australians and unaffected by the decision. The rest was Crown land, including great swathes of the outback leased to pastoralists and mining companies. Aboriginal leaders immediately announced that they would launch a stream of claims to seek native title to this land.

It looked as if the Vesteys had seen all this coming and the sale of their properties in the 1980s had been a shrewd decision. But the real reason lay elsewhere. At Vestey headquarters in London it had begun to dawn on the family that something was going wrong with their global operations. Their reaction was half-hearted – a sale of assets here and there, some rationalisation, more cost-cutting measures. It was to be too little, too late.

12

The Vesteys Today

Murder, divorce and disaster

Until the Vesteys' tax avoidance schemes brought them to public notice in 1980–81, little was known about them because the present generation maintained the family's obsession with secrecy. Lord Vestey, in a rare interview with the *Financial Times* in 1972, announced that the Vesteys had kept themselves to themselves for eighty years and saw no reason to change. As Jane Cadzow, an Australian journalist who wrote about the family's Australian connections, said, 'The Vesteys loathe publicity and would rather chew glass than discuss their affairs with outsiders.' *Tatler* writer Anthony Gardner also noticed the Vesteys' secretive ways: 'The Vesteys make the Freemasons look like chatterboxes.'

Lord Vestey had made it plain on many occasions that he detested the press. On a visit to Australia in 1972 he told a Melbourne journalist, 'You're just a tin-pot little reporter from a local paper. I don't have to see you. I'm a busy man. You'll have to pull your socks up, chappie.' Twenty years later his attitude had not changed. When

Anthony Gardner went to see him, Lord Vestey was the model of courtesy until there was a mix-up over a return appointment. Then Lord Vestey told him, 'You are the most disgusting little shit I have ever come across . . . How dare you come bursting into my office without an invitation? Do I have the right of veto on this article? No? Out! Out! . . . You'd better bloody well get it right, sonny, or I'll sue you until your feet don't touch the ground.'

But, even without publicity, it became obvious during the 1980s that Lord Vestey and his cousin, Edmund, who ran the Vestey empire jointly, were very different men from their ancestors. Neither William nor the first Edmund had any consuming interests outside their business. William's descendants became polo enthusiasts; Edmund's were drawn by hunting. Lord Vestey's interest in polo began when he was doing his National Service with the Scots Guards and was posted to Kenya. He played again in Australia and Argentina when out there learning the business. He told friends that the game meant a lot to him because it took his mind off work: 'After a hard day at the office there is nothing quite like it. When you're riding a horse and trying to hit a ball at the same time, you've no time to think about anything else.'

Lord Vestey and his younger brother, Mark, ran two successful teams, Stowell Park, after Lord Vestey's Gloucestershire home, and Foxcote, after Mark Vestey's house, Foxcote Manor. At one time or another, the two teams won every high-goal trophy on offer. Lord Vestey had a three-goal handicap, Mark Vestey four. But their teams were helped by two leading Argentine players, the late Eduardo Moore, who was a ten-goal handicap player, and the late Hector Barrantes, eight-goal handicap, who would come to Stowell Park to play for the Vesteys. At

Stowell Park they were Lord Vestey's guests and each was given a car for the length of his stay. During this period little seemed to matter to the Vesteys other than polo. Lord Vestey's large staff at Stowell Park included a polo manager and at one time he had a helicopter to fly him between his home, his office and Cirencester Park Polo Club.

He was a member of Whites, Jockey (Newmarket) and the Melbourne Club. He became chairman of the Cheltenham racecourse and was once Chief Disciplinary Steward of the Jockey Club. He gambled, usually favouring punto banco. When he entertained he did so lavishly and his guest lists were wide-ranging. A polo ball at Stowell Park in 1980 was attended by Prince Charles and some of his friends, their privacy being ensured by an expensive team of security guards. He drove a Range Rover with a number plate beginning SAM and his garage included a 1950s MG in perfect condition, a collector's item.

Edmund Vestey became joint master of the Puckeridge and Thurlow Foxhounds, near his home – Waltons, Ashdon, Saffron Walden, Essex – and in the season he hunted two or three days a week. He was High Sheriff of Essex in 1977 and in 1980 was Deputy Lieutenant of the county. He was a member of the Cavalry and Guards, Carlton and Highland (Inverness). With his family – he married Anne Moubray, the youngest daughter of General Sir Geoffrey Scoones, in 1960 – he spent most of his time at Waltons. But he had two other addresses, Sunnyside Farmhouse, Hawick, Roxburghshire, and the 100,000-acre estate at Assynt, Sutherland, Scotland.

This estate, on the Atlantic coast of the north-west, originally belonged to Edmund's father, Ronald Vestey, who bought it from the Westminster–Grosvenor estate.

Edmund added to it by buying 13,000 acres for £105,000 from Kildonan estates in 1956. In 1960, Ronald began signing over the estate to Edmund and there was a mixture of ownership between them. From 1966 to 1980, the period when capital transfer tax would have fallen due, Ronald handed over to Edmund ownership of the entire estate. But the tax, which could have been as high as £1 million, was not demanded because the Treasury gave the Vesteys exemption from paying it on the grounds that the estate was part of the national heritage, being of 'outstanding scenic interest'. The exemption had two conditions: the Vesteys could not develop the land without consulting conservation bodies, and they had to allow the public reasonable access.

Ronald Vestey lived in some style at Great Thurlow Hall, Suffolk. The house had a staff that included a cook, butler, secretary, chauffeur, gamekeepers, gardeners and maintenance men. There was a private pheasant shoot, a trout lake, a swimming pool and a deck quoits area. Until he was in his early eighties, Ronald Vestey still went to the Smithfield offices on Tuesdays, Wednesdays and Thursdays, driving up to the outskirts of London in his Rolls Royce and then changing to an Austin 1800 so that his staff would not think him ostentatious with his wealth. He inspected his property on Fridays, went shooting on Saturdays and to church on Sundays. He gave generously to local charities, matching what the charity could raise pound for pound. He donated £200,000 to the cathedral in Bury St Edmunds in memory of his wife, Florence, who died in 1966. He, too, was a former High Sheriff of Suffolk and a Deputy Lieutenant of the county.

To their relief, the 1980 storm over the Vesteys' tax arrangements blew over fairly quickly and they might well have been able to retreat into their private world had not a series of newsworthy disasters hit the family. It began in 1981 with Lord Vestey's divorce. In 1970 he had married Kate Eccles, the daughter of a director of the Heinz group, and they had two children, Saffron and Flora. But the marriage was soon in difficulty. Lord Vestey desperately wanted an heir but his wife did not provide one. Kate was a lover of ballet and opera; Lord Vestey cared for neither. Kate enjoyed fashionable restaurants and fine food; Lord Vestey ate out only when he had to and preferred plain food to 'mucked-up grub'. She preferred the city; he the country. She was a late 20th-century woman; he said once that he was a feudalist and that he did not know what Women's Lib meant.

The fear that their children might be targets for terrorists traumatised them both. As mentioned in Chapter 7, the Vesteys had ransomed Ronald Grove, their manager in Argentina, when guerrillas kidnapped him in 1972, so they took the threat to Saffron and Flora very seriously. Then Kate had a relationship with Lord Vestey's polo professional, Eduardo Moore. A fifteen-month separation from Lord Vestey followed and in 1981 the couple were finally divorced, Kate receiving a settlement running to millions of pounds.

Later that year Lord Vestey married Celia Knight, a nurse. He had met her four months earlier at a dance at Buckingham Palace – 'quite a good throwaway line, isn't it?' he says. They have two sons, William and Arthur, so Lord Vestey now has the heir he wanted. Celia – Cece to her circle – is a friend of the Princess of Wales and is Prince Harry's godmother, so at weekends the Vesteys would often entertain the Waleses, along with the Westminsters, the Beauforts, the Astors, the Hoares and the Cobbolds. It would be hard to name a better-connected family.

Then in 1984, while trying out a new horse with the Heythrop hunt, Mark Vestey hit a fence, fell off and broke his back. Paralysed from the waist down, he has been confined to a wheelchair ever since. Generally recognised as the nicest of the Vesteys, Mark refused to allow his accident to curtail his active life. He continued to play his part in the business, followed the hunt in an adapted Range Rover, and even managed to shoot, using a swivelling office chair manoeuvred by his wife, Rosie. He became chairman of Cirencester Park Polo Club and encouraged his children, two daughters and a son, to play. But Mark's accident had a devastating effect on Lord Vestey. He not only stopped playing polo, but also refused to watch it. One friend claimed that he even gave up drinking because 'he felt that it was a sacrifice which would cost him a lot and he wanted to suffer with his brother'. *Tatler* later published a moving photograph of Lord Vestey's once highly-successful polo team, showing Lord Vestey with Mark (now crippled), Hector Barrantes (died from cancer) and Eduardo Moore (committed suicide).

The very same year, Lord Vestey's cousin, Australian-born Michael Telling, thirty-four, was tried for the murder of his American wife, Monika. The hearing, in Exeter Crown Court, Devon, attracted reporters from all over the world. There was evidence of a headless corpse, lesbianism, drugs, alcohol, insanity, depravity, and even a pet cockatoo whose squawked insults were cited as proof of mental cruelty. Telling told of a traumatic childhood when his mother, a granddaughter of the first Lord Vestey, was married to hard-drinking Henry Telling, a Vestey director.

Michael, starved of affection, ran wild and spent years in homes for disturbed children.

At eighteen he had received his share-out from one of the Vestey family trusts and indulged his passion for motorcycles. Riding a Harley Davidson in San Francisco in 1980, he had met Monika Zumsteg and married her the following year. But, he said, not long after they moved to Britain, he found Monika embracing a woman neighbour on the lounge-room floor. On holiday in Austria, he caught Monika in bed with another woman, the wife of a solicitor. He said that Monika would belittle him in front of their friends and refer disparagingly to his sexual performance. Monika attacked him several times, once firing a gun at him, and on another occasion trying to run him down with a car. Telling attacked her too, four times, but in March 1984 they attempted a reconciliation.

Telling said that this failed when Monika began nagging him to go into a mental hospital, so he shot her three times. Then he hid the body in a half-finished sauna for five months, often visiting it, and, he claimed, kissing it. Finally he dumped Monika's remains in a wooded beauty spot near Exeter, chopped off her head with an axe 'because I wanted to take something of her back with me', and kept it in the boot of his car. Telling was found guilty of manslaughter on the grounds of diminished responsibility and jailed for life.

The trial was fodder for the British press which, by the end of it, had not only firmly linked Michael to the rest of the Vestey family but had translated the sauna into a deep freeze and implied that Michael's beheading of the corpse and putting it in cold storage was in the best tradition of a meat-producing family, 'a ghoulish come-uppance' which might have been devised for them by the horror writer Roald Dahl.

Then in 1987 Ronald died, aged eighty-nine, leaving an estate valued at £6,060,243 net. Ronald's death marked the end of a decisive era for the Vesteys. Although he had not taken an active role in the business for years, his presence and his example continued to dominate the Vestey thinking. Many observers believed him to be the most important member of the family. 'Sam and William may have made the Vesteys rich,' said one, 'but it was Ronald who made them mega-rich.' It was Ronald who emphasised that it was a *family* business, that it should be run by the family, each member of which should be knowledgeable about the tiniest detail of the operation. It was impossible to run such a huge business without employees but even the most trusted should be kept at arm's length and subjected to the same principle adopted in the intelligence community, that of 'need to know': each employee should be told only sufficient to enable him to do his job. So very few of the group's thousands of employees knew the true extent of the empire, or apparently, even the real size of individual operating companies.

Employees should be treated fairly but without sentiment. It was Vestey policy, for example, to promote three times a good workman in their Argentine packing plants. But when the man became due for a fourth promotion, he was sacked on the grounds that he had already given his best for the company and now could only decline. Managers in Australia were rewarded not on the profit they made but on their expenditure – the lower they kept costs, the higher their salary. No outside agencies should be employed if it was possible to do the job 'in-house', that is within the Vestey empire. This no doubt worked when the family had the fierce single-mindedness of William, the first Edmund and Ronald, but as we have seen, Edmund and the present Lord Vestey had other interests in life and, anyway, the empire had grown too big.

All they needed to have done was to have employed some competent professionals to help and to have paid them an attractive salary. But this went against the Vestey grain. In the late 1970s, when the Vesteys' main company, Union Cold Storage, had some 24,000 employees, few earned more than £12,000 a year. As a result, the family failed to attract top men. 'Most of the senior executives seem to be ex-guards officers hired by Sam,' one observer noted. This was at a time when Union Cold Storage had a bank overdraft of nearly £50 million and really needed experts to handle its treasury functions. One adviser told the family, 'Look, if you insist on doing everything in-house, then why not buy a merchant bank to look after your finance for you?' They declined his suggestion. In short, when the crash came, one City critic said that the family had been 'living in a time warp'.

13

Decade of Decline

The banks move in

Ronald Vestey never forgot that the family's core business was selling meat – we have seen how carefully he watched the Dewhurst butcher shops, visiting them regularly, often in disguise, eavesdropping on customers' conversations, always alert for any shifts in consumer demand. But the present generation took their eye off the meat business. They underestimated the effect that the European Community's beef mountain would have on Britain. Despite 'give away' sales to Russia and Mexico, by 1992 the 600,000 tons of beef in the EC stockpile began to cast a heavy shadow over British prices. The Vesteys' 1,000 butcher shops in Britain, the Dewhurst chain, had prospered by selling large quantities of cheap meat. But now the era of the meat kings was over as the ubiquitous supermarkets began to undercut them, and the habits of the British housewife underwent a revolution. Why make a separate trip to the high street butcher shop when she could buy everything – including her meat – at the supermarket, especially when it sold meat already prepared for the dish she was planning? 'Dewhurst had been woefully managed,' said a meat industry expert. 'It had too many shops, it needed re-positioning, and it did not offer enough high-margin, value-added products.'

Yet at the very time when the Vesteys should have been devoting all their attention to these problems, they were diversifying into areas where they lacked the same expertise that had made them successful in the meat. One, in particular, was disastrous. They plunged into speculation in commercial property. The Vesteys had always owned property, ranging from the pastoral land on which they raised their cattle, to their high street butcher shops. What altered now was that they began to buy and develop property outside their group of companies.

In Central London they began three office developments at the peak of the market: one in St John's Lane and one in West Smithfield, both close to Union's head office, and one in Leadenhall Street in the former head office of Vesteys' Blue Star shipping line. Outside London they developed a large office block in Cambridge. There was strong opposition to these ventures from the family's advisers, but they went ahead regardless. The subsequent slump in commercial property forced the Vesteys to write down the value of their unlet property developments by more than £60 million. So from about the mid-1980s they began to drip-feed Union with family assets.

In 1986 Union bought a family company, Commercial Properties, in exchange for shares valued at £65.5 million. In 1988 a second family company, New Holding and Finance, valued at £58 million, was inserted into Union. Despite this, in all but one of the years from 1984 until 1990, Union derived most of its profits from selling off assets: £23 million's worth in 1984, rising to £100 million's worth in 1990.

Two experts on the *Financial Times*, John Plender and Michiyo Nakamoto, analysed Union's balance sheet over this period and explained what had happened. 'At the start of 1985, Union had shareholders' funds, including minority interests, of just under £100 million. By the end of 1990, the comparable figure was £209 million. Yet in the interim, in a period when Union's core non-property business was profitable overall, the company had had the benefit of capital injection from family and outside sources of £222 million and surpluses on asset sales of £86 million. Somewhere along the way nearly £200 million disappeared from shareholders' funds in the balance sheet. [£100 million there in 1985 plus £222 million capital injection plus £86 million asset sales minus £209 million present in 1990 equals £199 million.]

'And while some of it can be straight-forwardly explained – for example by goodwill arising on acquisitions, capital redemptions, taxation and £23 million of dividends paid to Western United [another Vestey company], more than half represents a genuine loss of value. The key to the black hole in Union's balance sheet lies in the movements on reserves where much of the fall-out from hyper-inflation in the group's Latin American business winds up. So, too, does the fall-out from currency depreciation in Australia and New Zealand.

'Every year Union records in its balance sheet huge positive inflation adjustments and huge negative exchange rate adjustments. The net impact is always the same: a massive erosion of reserves, amounting to no less than £117 million over the past seven years. In other words, a family meat empire once regarded as an invincible money-making machine appears to have turned into a massive drain on the family's capital resources.' The *Financial Times* concluded that the exchange rate problem could actually dwarf the property problem.

In June, 1991 the family tried a change in leadership. Six months earlier, when discussing the running of Union, Edmund Vestey had said of his second cousin, Sam, 'We both look after various bits on a day-to-day basis. He looks after what I looked after ten years ago when my father [Ronald] was at the helm. I now look after the retail side of the meat business, fish, fruit, cold storage, insurance and shipping. We are partners and when I retire he will become chairman.' But that did not happen. Instead, in what some insiders described as a *coup d'état* rather than a handover, Edmund's son, Tim, then just thirty, said to be worth £250 million in his own right, took over as chief executive. When Tim was asked about Lord Vestey, he replied that he barely knew him until 1983. 'We live in Essex. He lives in Gloucestershire . . . I think we get on well.' What would Lord Vestey be doing under Tim's new regime? He would have 'an ambassadorial role'. Tim said that he had got the top job because the shareholders had asked him to do it. Whether his appointment came as a result of a family disagreement on Union's future is not known. But one thing was clear – Tim was in. Edmund and Sam had been relegated to the sidelines.

Tim Vestey's first public role was not a happy one. In October 1991 he had to announce that Union was heading for a breach of its borrowing covenants, which required that its pre-tax profits should be twice its interest payments. He immediately called a crisis meeting of Union's bankers. Representatives of some seventy banks, owed about £423 million, most of it unsecured, by Union (which had net assets of about £130 million – admittedly a very conservative figure), turned up at the Whitbread Brewery in London. There they listened in dismay as Tim told them that the Vesteys wanted them to approve a programme to re-finance more than £100 million of short-term debt while the company pursued a cost-cutting and disposal-of-assets programme. It was not an attractive offer, requiring as it did a double leap of faith by the banks. Firstly they had to believe that the currency depreciation which had got Union into trouble in the first place was at an end, or that Union's businesses in weak currency countries could be sold off without damaging the company balance sheet. And they had to believe that the Vestey management was not only capable of returning Union to profit but of generating sufficient profit to stop the continuing erosion of Union's capital base. The alternative to believing either of these propositions – that of putting Union into administration – was vigorously discouraged by Tim. 'I argued that this would not serve their interests well at all because it would impose instabilities that are totally unattractive,' he said later.

At a series of meetings over the next two months, the banks realised that although there was something piquant about the super-rich Vesteys coming to them with a begging bowl, the Vesteys nevertheless had the upper hand. The banks had lent generously to Union in the belief that the Vestey fortune stood behind the company, only to be told now that the family did not believe that further injection of their own capital was the solution to Union's problems. The bankers were stunned. One said, 'We thought the loans were rock solid because we believed that the Vesteys would stand behind their own company. They put about £170 million into Union over the past ten years so we thought it inconceivable that such an enormously rich family would not put in more. How wrong can you be? We were badly let down.' The British banks took it with a stiff upper lip but the Australian banks, Westpac and ANZ, quickly turned nasty. A British observer present at one meeting reported, 'I never thought I'd hear language like that between banker and client. You'd certainly never get it in Britain. We don't have ugly banks. But Tim Vestey had to sit there and listen to direct and very colourful Antipodean abuse. Basically the Australians were demanding to know why they should believe a single word he said.'

The Australians' anger seemed to have some effect. To keep the banks on board, the Vesteys agreed in January, 1992 to pump a final £40 million of family money into Union and to bring in an outsider to run the company. 'There was a strong feeling that since it was the Vesteys who got us into this mess, they were not the best ones to get us out,' one banker said. The man chosen was Terry Robinson, a former finance director of the giant multi-national, Lonrho, and the leader of its successful defence against a take-over bid in the mid-1980s from the Australian entrepreneur, Alan Bond. (Robinson plied bankers, media and investors with revelations about Mr Bond's enormous debts – 'he is technically insolvent' – and questionable business activities. Bond's financial standing never recovered and his empire collapsed not long afterwards.)

Robinson took over as chief executive of Union, above Tim Vestey, and 'with the approval of Union's principal bankers', as the company's statement put it. Robinson himself frankly admitted that his role would be 'to keep the banks happy'. In short, Union had been effectively taken away from the Vesteys and was being run by the banks' man, a humiliating situation for such a close family operation. Robinson had no illusions about his task. 'I see it as a three-year programme,' he said. 'It is more than just a challenge; it is making something out of a desperate situation . . . I want to look at all the operations before deciding on disposals. Everything is up for review, and businesses that cannot stand on their own two feet will be high on the list of likely sales.'

Among the first to go was the remainder of the Vesteys' Australian operation. In Brisbane on June 24, 1992, in one of the largest land sales in the nation's history, nine Vestey cattle stations went to auction, the final dismantling of an empire founded when Evelene made her dash to Australia to sign land leases seventy-five years earlier. On offer were Wave Hill and Cattle Creek (one lot) and Helen Springs in the Northern Territory, and Morstone Downs, Oban, Coolullah, Lake Learmouth, Fitzroy Vale and Archer in Queensland. Six realised $37.55 million at the auction and the remaining three properties were sold the following month.

Although one property, Fitzroy Vale, was bought by the Greek shipping magnate Gregory Hadjieleftheriadis, all the other buyers were Australian individuals or companies. The Vesteys, whose cattle stations in Australia had once covered an area bigger than Europe, had gone for ever; the locals had 'bought back the farm'.

In Britain the chill wind of recession made it hard for Union. The last thing Robinson wanted was a fire sale so he made it clear early on that Union would only sell where the proper opportunity presented itself. But six of Union's seven European branches had already been closed and a pork abattoir and an insurance broking business sold. There were other dividends. By late 1992 Robinson was able to say that with help from the banks and the application of group management and divisional management Union had 'substantially stabilised' and that the three-year re-financing plan was on schedule. At Smithfield, life at Vestey headquarters, known to some employees as 'the Kremlin', had become even more spartan than Ronald could have imagined. Although the offices, with their photographs of old freighters and warehouses, seemed unchanged since the First World War, Jeff Randall, City editor of the *Sunday Times*, was taken aback when Tim Vestey and Terry Robinson sat him down to a lunch that consisted of a small plate of sandwiches, 'served without wine, beer or even a bottle of water'. He was impressed with Robinson's drive but considered that the future of Union was by no means assured. 'Unlike the Vesteys, Robinson will not be given a second chance,' he wrote. 'Unless Union responds swiftly to his surgery, one of Britain's biggest and oldest private companies will be put into administration.'

By the summer of 1993 this seemed unlikely. The company had reported a profit before tax and exceptional items of £30.8 million for the year ending 31 December, compared with a loss of £20.5 million the previous year. But there were rumblings within the organisation. In June, the Vesteys, who appeared to have accepted their loss of power with equanimity, sprang a surprise. They announced that they had decided to establish a new management company to which all group operations and investments would report, including Union and Terry Robinson. The new company would be headed not by Lord Vestey, or Edmund Vestey, or even Tim Vestey, but by a new chief executive and chief financial officer. The Vesteys said they they were looking for the right man to hire. Where did this leave Robinson, who had quickly made it clear that he was not prepared in the short term to report to any new management company? The *Financial Times*, under the heading 'The empire strikes back', said perhaps Robinson had been too sharply critical of the Vestey family regime to be deemed a trusty retainer.

Either way, the Vesteys' recognition that they needed outside help may have come too late to restore their business empire to its previous financial pinnacle. If so, where would this leave the Vesteys themselves?

William, Edmund and Ronald Vestey worked during their lifetime to insulate the family from the ups and downs of fortune and from what they saw as the cupidity of governments. They planned a financial strategy for 100 years, they set down business procedures and investment policies, and they established a line of succession within the family that they hoped would avoid debilitating quarrels. What they did not foresee was that the food industry would not be able to keep up the high rates of return it had in the past and that Union would, as a result, find itself in deep trouble.

This altered predictions of how great the Vestey fortune would be if the family continued to allow their trust fund to accumulate for the whole lifetime of the trust, until the year 2030. In 1981, calculations based on a modest three per cent annual growth applied to the family's wealth that year, a conservative £924 million, produced a figure of £3,933 million. At seven per cent annual growth, the figure was a staggering £25,437.62 million. These figures have to be revised. Best estimates now suggest that if the Vesteys were able to realise in 1993 all the wealth accumulated in all their trusts they would be worth a conservative £1,317 million. If they were to wait until 2030 the figure would be £4,172 million.

Of course, there is much that could occur to make the latter figure wrong. Some future British government might decide that it was not desirable that a large part of the British food industry should remain in the control of a single family and launch an anti-monopoly action. There could be new tax legislation which the Vesteys considered insupportable. When the family was in the public eye in 1981, Edmund Hoyle Vestey justified the Vesteys' tax schemes by saying that faced with the choice of going bankrupt or 'shifting out', they had opted for the overseas trusts. This raises the question of whether, if the Inland Revenue were ever seriously to concern the family again, the Vestey group might leave Britain altogether. Certainly at one stage their organisation had a contingency plan to cope with the threat of nationalisation, new tax laws, or an anti-monopoly action. The plan set out in great detail how everything could legally be moved out of Britain within twenty-four hours. One day the Vesteys would be here – Britain's richest family, friends of Royalty, pillars of the establishment. By the morning they would be gone.

But everything suggests that now the Vesteys would never consider such a move. They are too British. (And where would they go? There is no Empire any more.) They have frequently expressed their patriotism and have served in the armed forces in both war and peace. They are proud of the fact that they brought cheap meat to the masses and provided employment for thousands. And their reaction to their difficulties with Union suggests that not only had they learnt from the experience but that they were capable of fighting back. While Lord Vestey and Edmund were looking for a high-powered, outside professional to take care of all the family interests – something their critics said they should have done years ago – young Tim Vestey was studying at business school, to be ready if necessary to take over the top job himself one day. So although the House of Vestey may have declined, it is too early to write it off. That is another thing about seriously rich families: they do not let go easily.

Index